ChLA

THE PHOENIX AWARD
of
The Children's Literature Association

1985-1989

edited by

Alethea Helbig and Agnes Perkins

The Scarecrow Press, Inc.
Metuchen, N.J., & London
1993

PS
490
.P48
1993

British Library Cataloguing-in-Publication data available

Library of Congress Cataloging-in-Publication Data

The Phoenix Award of the Children's Literature Association,
    1985-1989 / edited by Alethea Helbig and Agnes Perkins.
        p.   cm.
    Includes bibliographical references.
    ISBN 0-8108-2677-1 (acid-free paper)
    1. Children's literature, American—History and criticism.
2. Children's literature, English—History and criticism. 3.
Children's literature—Authorship. 4. Literary prizes—United
States. 5. Phoenix Award. I. Helbig, Alethea. II. Perkins,
Agnes. III. Children's Literature Association (U.S.)
PS490.P48 1993
810.9' 9282—dc20   93-12580

Copyright © 1993 by Alethea Helbig and Agnes Perkins
Manufactured in the United States of America
Printed on acid-free paper

Contents

Foreword	vii
Introduction	xi
The Winners and the Honor Books of The Children's Literature Association Phoenix Award, 1985-1989	3
The 1985 Phoenix Award Winner: *The Mark of the Horse Lord* **by Rosemary Sutcliff**	5
Acceptance / *Rosemary Sutcliff*	7
Biographical Sketch of Rosemary Sutcliff	9
Books by Rosemary Sutcliff	11
Rosemary Sutcliff's *The Mark of the Horse Lord* and Roman Trilogy / *Agnes Perkins*	15
Life, Death, and Honor in Rosemary Sutcliff's *Sun Horse, Moon Horse* and *Warrior Scarlet* / *Mary Weichsel Ake*	18
Dawn Wind and *Knight's Fee*: Two Medieval Novels by Rosemary Sutcliff / *M. Sarah Smedman*	21
Heroic Literature by Rosemary Sutcliff / *Alethea Helbig*	27

The 1986 Phoenix Award Winner:
Queenie Peavy by Robert Burch 33

Acceptance / *Robert Burch* 35
Biographical Sketch of Robert Burch 39
Books by Robert Burch 41
Three Problem Novels that Hold Up /
   Rebecca Lukens 43
Robert Burch's Forte: Books Laid in Rural
   Georgia / *Mary Weichsel Ake* 47
Family Harmony and Love of Life in Four
   Books by Robert Burch / *M. Sarah Smedman* 50
Four Mid-Seventies Books by Robert Burch /
   Mark I. West 53
Moral Issues Confronted / *Alethea Helbig* 56

The 1987 Phoenix Award Winner:
Smith by Leon Garfield 61

Acceptance / *Leon Garfield* 63
Biographical Sketch of Leon Garfield 65
Books by Leon Garfield 67
Mystery and Melodrama: Three Novels by
   Leon Garfield / *Agnes Perkins* 71
Comedy and Social History in Books by
   Leon Garfield / *Mark I. West* 75
Retellings from Greek Mythology and Picture
   Book Stories by Leon Garfield / *Taimi M. Ranta* 77
Leon Garfield's Ghost Stories / *Alethea Helbig* 83

The 1988 Phoenix Award Winner:
The Rider and His Horse
by Erik Christian Haugaard 89

Acceptance / *Erik Christian Haugaard* 91
Biographical Sketch of Erik Christian Haugaard 95
Books by Erik Christian Haugaard 97

Diversity and Consistency in Erik Haugaard's Novels / *Agnes Perkins*	99
Haugaard's Norse Tales / *Mark I. West*	102
The Condemnation of War in Three of Haugaard's Books for Young People / *Taimi M. Ranta*	104
On Three Works by Erik Haugaard: *Prince Boghole, A Boy's Will,* and *Orphans of the Wind* / *E. Wendy Saul*	110
The English Civil War Novels of Erik Christian Haugaard / *Alethea Helbig*	114

The 1989 Phoenix Award Winner: *The Night Watchmen* by Helen Cresswell

	119
Acceptance / *Helen Cresswell*	121
Biograpical Sketch of Helen Cresswell	125
Books by Helen Cresswell	127
Magic at the Edges: An Appreciation of *The Night Watchmen* / *Mark I. West*	131
The Bagthorpe Saga of Helen Cresswell, or What Happens When Eccentricity Becomes the Norm / *Millicent Lenz*	134
Playing with Convention: Four Novels by Helen Cresswell / *Alethea Helbig*	139

1989 Phoenix Award Honor Book: *Brother, Can You Spare a Dime?* by Milton Meltzer

	145
Biographical Sketch of Milton Meltzer	147
Books by Milton Meltzer	149
Milton Meltzer's *Brother, Can You Spare a Dime?*: A Study in Passionate Fact / *E. Wendy Saul*	153

1989 Phoenix Award Honor Book:
  Pistol by Adrienne Richard   157

  Biographical Sketch of Adrienne Richard   159
  Books by Adrienne Richard   161
  Pistol: End of an Era, Beginning of Another /
    Taimi M. Ranta   163

About the Editors   167

Foreword

"Has it really been twenty years since I wrote about Queenie?" Robert Burch mused at the banquet honoring him for *Queenie Peavy* (Viking, 1966). Years slip away and Burch, like the rest of us, was surprised at the passing of time.

Time is an important part of what the Phoenix Award is about. The Phoenix came into being in 1985, but it had been in a long gestation period before that. Alethea Helbig, Agnes Perkins, Mary Ake, among others, deliberated long about the importance of children's books and their lasting effect on us. Over the years they put together a plan to honor a book published twenty years earlier that had not received a major award on publication but which is recognized now by specialists of children's literature to be exemplary. These books have stood the test of time. They have unusually high artistic merit and are of such universal themes and appeal that they are as relevant today as they were a generation earlier. Superior children's books have this kind of lasting effect, and this volume pays tribute to the first five Phoenix Award winners.

The first award was given in 1985 to *The Mark of the Horse Lord* (Oxford, 1965) by Rosemary Sutcliff. She tells the story of Midir, the prince of a tribal group in Scotland in the second century. At fourteen he had been beaten, blinded, and left for dead. Liadhan, the villainous woman responsible for Midir's maiming and the death of his father, then ruled his people because a blind king was unacceptable. Years passed.

Phaedrus, a slave recently released from the gladiatorial arena, bears a striking likeness to Midir and is encouraged by a small group of loyal supporters to take Midir's place as king. Phaedrus meets Midir, admires him, and agrees. He is branded with the mark of the king, trained extensively by a select group of warriors who will keep the secret, and escorted north to Scotland to rule Midir's people.

Sutcliff's language, mood, and tone take us into the smells, noises, and even the fears of ancient Scotland as this novel follows one absorbing adventure with another until the final chilling scene. Charles Keeping's black and white illustrations help intensify the drama and mood.

Queenie Peavy by Robert Burch is the 1986 winner. It is set in rural Georgia in the 1930s. Queenie is thirteen, perceived by almost everyone as a brat. Even those who understand her struggle with a poor self-image are hard pressed to know how to coax Queenie into being her own best self. She is smart and likes school, but she also throws rocks with deadly accuracy, and she chews and spits tobacco. Her story is one of painful recognition of her own limitations fused with her growing understanding of her own potential. Burch's voice is right on target with this story of poverty and neglect, so that we are able to be part of Queenie's rebellion and her growing acceptance of herself as she faces her problems with candor and courage.

The 1987 winner, Leon Garfield's *Smith* (Constable, 1967) takes readers into nineteenth-century England with one of the most beguiling characters of literature. Smith is a filthy, twelve-year-old pickpocket who lives by his wits on the streets of London. He cannot read, has no parents, and is trusted by no one—for good reason. Within the first six pages Smith inadvertently witnesses a murder; the remaining pages are devoted to the avoiding of his own murder. He befriends blind old Mr. Mansfield who is the victim of ruffians. The meeting is plausible, and Mr. Mansfield takes Smith to his home to live.

Garfield uses words sparingly and exquisitely as he describes, for example, Miss Mansfield's reaction to her father's largesse. Her eyes are not blinded, and she sees Smith for the street urchin he is. Anthony Maitland's pen-and-ink illustrations add to the sense of the mystery, gloom, and despair of the London that was familiar to Smith.

The Rider and His Horse (Houghton Mifflin, 1968) by Erik Christian Haugaard is the 1988 winner. It is set in Israel following the destruction of Jerusalem in 70 A.D. David is the only son of a wealthy wine merchant, and he is captured by bandits to be sold into slavery. David's escape, his sojourn in Jerusalem, and his final stand at the Masada take him from childhood to manhood. He comes to understand that people who put their faith in learning and truth have a quality which will outlive the Roman civilization that enslaves them. The Romans take direction from the entrails of birds; the Jews follow direction from the Torah. David also learns that poets, not soldiers, are those who determine history because their writing tells important truths and lives after they are long dead.

The 1989 winner is *The Night Watchmen* (Faber, 1969) by Helen Cresswell. It is a tale of a child's lonely recuperation from a long illness and his meeting of two strangers in his village who call themselves the night watchmen. They have come from nowhere and are in the village to gauge its "ticking." They also watch for the train which will take them to wherever. Henry becomes absorbed with these men. He finds out that "ticking" means to observe so closely that one can sense the mood of a place. Vivid detail and a chilling climax that endangers Henry's life are part of the lure of this novel.

In 1989, the Phoenix Committee determined that two additional books deserved recognition and named the first Phoenix Honor Books. *Brother, Can You Spare a Dime?* (Knopf, 1969) by Milton Meltzer is about the first four years of America's Great Depression. Historical events set the time, but tone is established by Meltzer as he tells about lives of ordinary people who were affected by loss of job, farm, home, and dignity. Black-and-white photographs and memorable statements from people who suffered these years show the way our country was in the 1930s, when it was on the brink of disaster. This is a close look at an important part of American history that shows readers how people faced overwhelming troubles.

Pistol (Little, Brown, 1969) by Adrienne Richard, the second 1989 Honor Book, is also set in the 1930s. In novel form, it tells about Billy Catlett's high school years, a critical time to face change and deprivation as youngsters did. In the first part of the story, Billy is a horse wrangler, working with cowboys in Great Plains, Montana. When the banks fail, his father leaves, and his older brother, Conrad, becomes alienated and bitter. The family's moving to a new and roaring camp town where men can find work building a new dam is not untypical of impoverished families during America's Great Depression. Strong characterization and sense of place make this a poignant sharing of Billy's adolescence.

Phoenix Award-winning books were first published twenty years prior to receiving their awards. Most will have to be searched for on library shelves; however, some are still in print, and *The Night Watchmen* was reprinted after receiving this prestigious award. The books represent varying genres and style; all give good solid reading enjoyment for anyone ten and older. The Phoenix Award not only affirms the importance of children's and adolescent literature; it emphasizes the lasting and classic nature of the best of it.

The stories we read in childhood are those we remember throughout our lives. Because of this, nowhere is quality more important than in literature for the young, and the Phoenix Award confirms this truth. Phoenix Committee members work year round reading books they find and those which other people nominate in order to determine the best. They have taken on a demanding task and done a splendid job. All award winners are excellent books; they deserve this honor.

Norma Hayes Bagnall, President
Children's Literature Association
May 31, 1991

Introduction

The Phoenix Award of The Children's Literature Association (ChLA) is given to the author, or the estate of the author, of a book for children published twenty years earlier, which did not win a major award at the time of its publication, but which, from the perspective of time, is deemed worthy of special recognition for its high literary quality.

This book brings together for the first time the acceptance speeches of the award-winning authors and the papers given about the award-winning books and the honor books (when named) from inception in 1985 through 1989, the award's first five years. The papers were delivered in the respective years at sessions of The Children's Literature Association annual conferences at Ann Arbor, Michigan; Kansas City, Missouri; Ottawa, Canada; Charleston, South Carolina; and Mankato, Minnesota. The acceptance talks were given at the annual banquets at the time the awards were presented. Also included here are lists of the writers' books for children and biographical information about the writers.

The Children's Literature Association, an international organization of teachers, scholars, librarians, editors, writers, illustrators, and parents interested in encouraging the serious study of children's literature, created the Phoenix Award as an outgrowth of the work of the Association's Touchstones committee.* The award, given to a book originally published in the English language, is intended to recognize books of merit, encourage publishers to continue to make them available, and suggest to readers that they identify and cherish those qualities that have given these books universality and timelessness.

---

* The ChLA Touchstones books are discussed in several volumes entitled *Touchstones: Reflections on the Best in Children's Literature,* ed. by Perry Nodelman and published by The Children's Literature Association and Purdue University.

The Phoenix Award is named after the fabled bird that periodically rose from its ashes with renewed life and beauty. Like the ancient bird, Phoenix books also rise from neglect and obscurity and once again enrich the lives of those who read them.

The Phoenix Award is represented by a two-dimensional, freestanding, brass medallion inscribed with the title and author of the year's winner. It was specifically designed for The Children's Literature Association by the noted twentieth-century illustrator Trina Schart Hyman, whose Caldecott Award illustrations accompany a retelling of St. George and the Dragon. The design was sculpted by Professor Diane Davis of Purdue University. Prof. Davis is a sculptor trained at Johnson Atelier and Technical Institute of Sculpture, Princeton. Each medallion is individually cast.

The recipients of the Phoenix Award, which was initiated in 1985, are chosen by an elected committee of ChLA members, who serve overlapping, four-year terms. The committee considers nominations made by members and others interested in promoting high critical standards in literature for children. From 1985 to 1989, the following ChLA members served at various times on the selection committee: Mary Weichsel Ake, Littleton, Colorado, Public Schools; Millicent Lenz, State University of New York—Albany; Rebecca Lukens, Miami University—Ohio; Peter Neumeyer, San Diego State University; Agnes Perkins, Eastern Michigan University; Taimi M. Ranta, Illinois State University; E. Wendy Saul, University of Maryland; M. Sarah Smedman, Moorhead State University; Mark I. West, University of North Carolina—Charlotte; and Alethea Helbig, Eastern Michigan University, Chair.

THE PHOENIX AWARD

The Winners and the Honor Books of The Children's Literature Association Phoenix Award 1985-1989

1985—*The Mark of the Horse Lord* by Rosemary Sutcliff (Oxford, 1965; Walck, 1965; Penguin, 1983)

1986—*Queenie Peavy* by Robert Burch (Viking, 1966; Dell Yearling, 1975; Puffin, 1987)

1987—*Smith* by Leon Garfield (Constable, 1967; Pantheon, 1967; Penguin, 1968; Dell Yearling, 1987)

1988—*The Rider and His Horse* by Erik Christian Haugaard (Houghton Mifflin, 1968)

1989—*The Night Watchmen* by Helen Cresswell (Faber, 1969; Macmillan, 1969; Aladdin, 1989)

Honor Books (1989)

Brother, Can You Spare a Dime? by Milton Meltzer (Knopf, 1969)

Pistol by Adrienne Richard (Little, Brown, 1969; 1989)

The 1985 Phoenix Award Winner

The Mark of the Horse Lord

Rosemary Sutcliff

Once in Roman Britain a gladiator named Phaedrus won his freedom and agreed to impersonate the king of a Scottish tribe. As Horse Lord, he led his people against the woman who had usurped the throne and came into inevitable conflict with the conquering Romans. An exciting historical novel of steadily increasing emotional intensity, *The Mark of the Horse of the Lord* combines excellent characterizations with a clear, compelling style, illuminates with sensitivity and understanding a complex and turbulent era, and perfectly blends problem and period.

Acceptance: 1985 Phoenix Award

Rosemary Sutcliff

Ladies and Gentlemen. I wish so much that I could be with you in person today, to thank the Phoenix Award Committee and to tell all of you how grateful and how deeply honored I feel that *The Mark of the Horse Lord* should have been chosen as the first book to receive this wonderful new award.

Horse Lord is one of my best-beloved books, amongst my own, and has remained so warmly living in my mind, though I have never re-read it, that when I heard that it had won an award for a book published twenty years ago, my first thought was "How lovely!!" But my second was "But it can't be anywhere near twenty years old; it's one of my quite *recent* books; there must be some mistake!" And I made all speed to get it out of the bookcase and look at the publication date, to make sure. And having got it out, of course I started reading it again.

Re-reading a book of my own is for me (and I imagine for most authors) a faintly nerve-wracking process, with all the fascination, but all the danger too, of returning to a place that one was happy in, a long time ago. There are the passages that make one think, "This is bad! This is overwritten. This is PURPLE! How did it ever get published?" Which is depressing to say the least of it. And there are the passages which make one think, "This is *good!* This is vivid and sensitive, I am sure I can't write like that now," which is even more depressing. There are passages of both kinds in *Horse Lord*, but I do think, coming to it again after so many years, that it has stood the test of time, and I enjoyed reading it except for the end, which tore my heart out just as it did when I wrote it.

I seem to have a tendency to sad or only half-happy endings, but none of the others are as starkly tragic as the end of *Horse Lord*. I didn't want it to be like that. When I started, I was not really sure that it was going to be, and hoped for the best. But as the book went on, its last page became more and more inevitable. I twisted and turned and tried all ways I could think of to find another way out, one that would save Red Phaedrus. But none of the endings I thought up rang true. They were all just manufactured happy endings that had really nothing to do with the story; and the tragic one, coming of its own accord, was the only one which belonged, which was organic to the story, completing the pattern which I had begun on the first page.

Quite a lot of friends and wellwishers told me, "You simply can't do that! Not in a children's book." But I don't believe that one should make allowances for young readers, feed them on pap. And children themselves show how little they need any punches pulled for them, by their fondness for both horror comics and the like, and for the ancient hero myths and legends which were certainly not meant for them in the first place, but of which they have taken possession, stories dealing with the big basic values (as, incidentally, the early Westerns did), love and hate, cowardice and courage, loyalty and divided loyalty, the quest for honor, above all, the unending struggle between Good and Evil, which almost always end tragically in the death of the hero, generally in his hour of victory. Children should be allowed the great themes, which are also often tragic themes, which they can receive and make use of better than most adults can.

Standing aside, myself, and speaking not as the author but simply as a looker on, I am so glad, too, that the first winner of the Phoenix Award should be a historical novel. There seems to be a feeling against the genre, nowadays, an idea that historical stories are simply escapist, and that because they are sited in the past, they have no relevance to the present day. In fact, of course, history and anything that helps to flesh out the bones of history and bring the past to life, has enormous relevance to the present day. To know where we started from and by what road we came to be where we are now—and to know this not only in an academic way but also with our emotions, not only with our heads but with our hearts, must surely be helping us in coping with the world in which we are today. And since history is a living and continuous process, must help us in our going forward into the part of history which is still in the future.

Once again, I give you my deepest thanks. I shall treasure my own particular phoenix, the first of its kind, as it deserves.

Rosemary Sutcliff

The first Children's Literature Association Phoenix Award was given to Rosemary Sutcliff, whom the many lovers of books for young people could easily agree was one of the best historical novelists of the twentieth century. In addition, she retold the stories of such heroic figures as Beowulf, Robin Hood, Cuchulain, Finn MacCool, Tristan and Iseult, Boadicea, and Arthur, always with the intensity and detail of fiction.

Sutcliff was born in 1920 in West Clanden, Surrey, the daughter of a naval officer, and the family moved frequently as he was stationed in a variety of places. Before she was three, she was afflicted by juvenile arthritis, a condition that recurred throughout her early years and left her crippled. She spent much of her childhood in hospitals, for operations and treatment. During one hospital stay she was awarded the Girl Guide Fortitude Badge, an honor that seems appropriate for her whole life in which she triumphed over physical handicaps, a lonely childhood, and an overprotective mother to lead a full and successful life.

At fourteen she left school to attend the Bideford School of Art in Devon, where she was persuaded by well-meaning adults to give up her ambition to become a full-scale artist and to turn her talents to painting miniatures, which they thought would be easier for her to handle. Although she became a skilled painter, had one of her works hung in the Royal Academy, and was named a member of the Royal Society of Miniature Painters, she was not fully committed to the discipline and began to write in secret. The first book she submitted to a publisher, a retelling of Saxon and Celtic legends, was rejected, but Oxford Press suggested that she write a Robin Hood for them.

Her earliest novels, like *Brother Dusty-Feet,* while accurate in history, have little character development, but in her Roman trilogy—*The Eagle of the Ninth, The Silver Branch,* and *The Lantern Bearers*—she developed the distinctive voice, memorable characters, and psychological depth that marked all her later fiction. With a few exceptions, her novels deal with the history of Britain, from the days before historical records to the English Civil War period. Frequently, her novels have a maimed or handicapped hero, and their themes concern the continuity of history and of peoples.

Of her retellings of hero tales, the three volumes of King Arthur—*The Sword and the Circle, The Light Beyond the Forest,* and *The Road to Camlann*—are the most substantial. An earlier foray into the Arthurian tales, *Sword at Sunset,* is written as a novel, picturing Arthur as he might have been historically, a Roman-British leader against invading Saxons. She retold the stories of Beowulf and Cuchulain with passion and excitement. Her *Tristan and Iseult* won the *Boston Globe-Horn Book* Award, and *Song for a Dark Queen* received the Children's Rights Workshop Other Award.

Among her other honors is the Carnegie Medal for *The Lantern Bearers. The Road to Camlann* was named a Junior High Contemporary Classic. Ten of her novels have been commended or highly commended by the Carnegie award committee, five have been named to the *Horn Book* Fanfare list, and one is on the Lewis Carroll Shelf. She was also named named a Fellow of the Royal Society of Literature and an Officer of the Order of the British Empire.

Rosemary Sutcliff died on July 22, 1992, in Chichester, Sussex, after a long and very distinguished literary career.

Books by Rosemary Sutcliff

The Chronicles of Robin Hood. Illus. C. Walter Hodges. London: Oxford, 1950; New York: Oxford, 1978.
The Queen Elizabeth Story. Illus. C. Walter Hodges. London: Oxford, 1950.
The Armourer's House. Illus. C. Walter Hodges. London and New York: Oxford, 1951.
Brother Dusty-Feet. Illus. C. Walter Hodges. London: Oxford, 1952.
Simon. Illus. Richard Kennedy. London: Oxford, 1953.
The Eagle of the Ninth. Illus. C. Walter Hodges. London: Oxford, 1954; New York: Walck, 1961.
Outcast. Illus. Richard Kennedy. London: Oxford, 1955; New York: Walck, 1955.
The Shield Ring. Illus. C. Walter Hodges. London: Oxford, 1956; New York: Walck, 1962.
The Silver Branch. Illus. Charles Keeping. London: Oxford, 1957; New York: Walck, 1959.
Warrior Scarlet. Illus. Charles Keeping. London: Oxford, 1958; New York: Walck, 1958.
The Lantern Bearers. Illus. Charles Keeping. London: Oxford, 1959; New York: Walck, 1959.
The Bridge-Builders. Oxford: Blackwell, 1959.
Houses and History. Illus. William Stobbs. London: Batsford, 1960.
Knight's Fee. Illus. Charles Keeping. London: Oxford, 1960; New York: Walck, 1960.
Beowulf. Illus. Charles Keeping. London: Bodley Head, 1961; New York: Dutton, 1962; as *Dragon Slayer.* London: Penguin, 1966.
Dawn Wind. Illus. Charles Keeping. London: Oxford, 1961; New York: Walck, 1962.
Sword at Sunset. London: Hodder and Stoughton, 1963; New York: Coward, 1964.
The Hound of Ulster. Illus. Victor Ambrus. London: Bodley Head, 1963; New York, Dutton, 1963.

A Saxon Settler. Illus. John Lawrence. London: Oxford, 1965.
Heroes and History. Illus. Charles Keeping. London: Batsford, 1965; New York: Dutton, 1965.
The Mark of the Horse Lord. Illus. Charles Keeping. London: Oxford, 1965; New York: Walck, 1965.
The Chief's Daughter. Illus. Victor Ambrus. London: H. Hamilton, 1967.
The High Deeds of Finn MacCool. Illus. Michael Charlton. London: Bodley Head, 1967; New York: Dutton, 1967.
A Circlet of Oak Leaves. Illus. Victor Ambrus. London: H. Hamilton, 1968.
The Flowers of Adonis. London: Hodder and Stoughton, 1969; New York: Coward, 1970.
The Witch's Brat. Illus. Robert Micklewright. London: Oxford, 1970; New York: Walck, 1970.
The Truce of the Games. Illus. Victor Ambrus. London: H. Hamilton, 1971.
Tristan and Iseult. Illus. Victor Ambrus. London: Bodley Head, 1971; New York: Dutton, 1971.
Heather, Oak, and Olive: Three Stories. Illus. Victor Ambrus. New York: Dutton, 1972.
The Capricorn Bracelet. Illus. Charles Keeping. London: Oxford, 1973; New York: Walck, 1973.
The Changeling. Illus. Victor Ambrus. London: H. Hamilton, 1974.
We Lived in Drumfyvie. With Margaret Lyford-Pike. London: Blackie, 1975.
Blood Feud. Illus. Charles Keeping. London: Oxford, 1977; New York: Dutton, 1977.
Shifting Sands. Illus. Laszlo Acs. London: H. Hamilton, 1977.
Sun Horse, Moon Horse. Illus. Shirley Felts. London: Bodley Head, 1977; New York: Dutton, 1978.
Song for a Dark Queen. London: Pelham, 1978; New York: Crowell, 1979.
The Light Beyond the Forest: The Quest for the Holy Grail. Illus. Shirley Felts. London: Bodley Head, 1979; New York: Dutton, 1980.
Frontier Wolf. London: Oxford, 1980; New York: Dutton, 1981.
Eagle's Egg. Illus. Victor Ambrus. London: H. Hamilton, 1981.

The Sword and the Circle: King Arthur and the Knights of the Round Table. Illus. Shirley Felts. London: Bodley Head, 1981; New York: Dutton, 1981.

The Road to Camlann: The Death of King Arthur. Illus. Shirley Felts. London: Bodley Head, 1981; New York: Dutton, 1982.

Bonnie Dundee. London: Bodley Head, 1983; New York: Dutton, 1984.

Blue Remembered Hills. London: Oxford, 1984.

The Roundabout Horse. Illus. Alan Marks. London: H. Hamilton, 1986.

Flame-Coloured Taffeta. London: Oxford, 1986; New York: Farrar, 1986.

A Little Dog Like You. Illus. Jane Johnson. London: Orchard, 1987; New York: Simon and Schuster, 1990.

Blood and Sand. London: Hodder and Stoughton, 1987.

Little Hound Found. Illus. Jo Davies. London: H. Hamilton, 1989.

The Shining Company. London: Bodley Head, 1990; New York: Farrar, 1990.

Rosemary Sutcliff's *The Mark of the Horse Lord* and Roman Trilogy

Agnes Perkins

Rosemary Sutcliff became well known and is still best remembered, at least in this country, for three books set in Roman times in Britain, connected by protagonists who share a family line and a ring passed down through the generations, although the stories span several hundred years. The first Phoenix Award goes this year to *The Mark of the Horse Lord*, another of her novels set while Rome controlled Britain. It differs in significant ways from the earlier Roman trilogy.

The Eagle of the Ninth is a historical adventure of an attempt to discover what happened to the Ninth Roman Legion which marched north into what is now Scotland in 17 A.D. and disappeared. Young Centurion Marcus Flavius Aquila, son of the second-in-command of the Legion, having been wounded and unable to serve in his former position, accepts the task of discovering whether there is any substance in rumors that the Eagle of the Ninth Legion is being used as a symbol to rally the northern tribes to rebellion. With his freed slave, a Briton named Esca, he travels north as a wandering physician, learns the truth of the doomed legion, recovers the Eagle, and makes a harrowing escape back south of the Roman wall.

The second book of the trilogy, *The Silver Branch,* is set in the last decade of the third century. Telling of the fall of Carausius, the self-proclaimed Emperor of Britain, it is essentially a spy story, in which two descendants of Marcus, both serving in the Roman forces, learn of the plot against Carausius but are unable to thwart it. After the Emperor is murdered, they become involved in an underground movement to sneak his supporters out of Britain and prepare the way for Constantius, who invades from Gaul to defeat the usurper, Allectus. It is a novel of intrigue and exciting action, with an underlying concern for what constitutes loyalty and heroism.

The Lantern Bearers, third in the trilogy, is a much more psychological novel. It is set in the early fifth century when the last of the Roman troops are recalled from Britain and the remaining British-Romans and Celts are left alone to repel invading Saxons. Young Aquila, commander of a cavalry unit, deserts before the galleys put out to sea and tries to defend his home farm. He sees his blind father killed, his beloved sister, Flavia, carried off, and is himself captured as a slave by raiders from Juteland. After three years, his master returns to Britain, taking Aquila with him. In a Saxon camp he comes upon Flavia, now married to her captor and mother of his son. She helps Aquila escape, but refuses to leave her husband and child. Bitterly, Aquila joins the forces of Ambrosius which are still trying to stem the tide of invasion and becomes a trusted member of the inner circle, but his private life is marred and almost destroyed by his inability to admit his affection for his wife and son, Minnow. When, after a major battle, he helps Flavia's son escape and Minnow stands up for him, he is at last able to come to terms with his sister's choice and to break through his own bitterness. Characterization in *The Lantern Bearers* is deeper than that in the two earlier novels, but the plot depends heavily upon coincidence.

The Mark of the Horse Lord, published nearly ten years later, is set about midpoint in the Roman period and is concerned with rivalries and wars among the northern tribes, beyond the direct control of the Legions. The gladiator, Red Phaedrus, born a slave, has won his liberty in an exhibition fight to the death against his one friend among the performers. Unable to handle freedom, he gets into a drunken street brawl and lands in jail. Agents for the Dalriad tribe, bent on wresting power from the Caledones and having seen his resemblance to their rightful king, Midir, bribe the guards and spirit him away to meet Midir, who has been blinded and horribly disfigured by his father's half-sister, the Caledone goddess-queen, who now rules both tribes. To get revenge, Midir coaches Phaedrus to take his place and lead an uprising which will free the Dalriads, worshipers of a male sun-god, from the Caledones, who worship the earth-mother moon goddess. His tense introduction to the Kindred, the royal clan, who accept him as the presumed-dead Midir, the ceremony of his king-making, his marriage to the Royal Daughter, and his intense involvement in the conflict with the Caledones are all shadowed constantly by the possibility that his true background may be discovered. In this role, he gradually changes from the shallow, flashy gladiator to a true king, responsible for his people and willing, in the end, to sacrifice himself to save them in their time of need.

This character change, subtly developed and convincing, is as deep and moving as that of Aquila in *The Lantern Bearers*. By facing coincidence squarely in the device of the look-alike, Sutcliff frees the rest of the plot from the unlikely chance meetings and overheard conversations which, though made to seem acceptable, are the greatest weaknesses in her other novels. Many scenes are memorable: the seven-year ritual slaying of the old king to renew the power of the goddess-queen and insure the health of the tribe, the ancient bride-hunt of the marriage ceremony which becomes a real hunt when the Royal Daughter tries to escape from Phaedrus, the night scene at the Roman fort in the rain and lightning when blind Midir kills the goddess-queen on the rampart stair. The book is rich in ironies and depths of meaning.

Sutcliff's greatest achievement, it seems to me, is to take a reader convincingly back into historical time without intrusive long descriptions or self-conscious inclusion of extraneous research. In *The Mark of the Horse Lord*, the sprawling Roman town where Phaedrus wins his wooden foil of freedom, the villages of the northern tribes, the war camps where Phaedrus at last reaches understanding and love with his young wife, the walled garrison where he makes his final, heroic decision—all these are more than backdrop setting, vivid with the color and smell and feel of the period. Secondary characters, Sinnoch, the horse merchant who bribes the jailers; Midir himself, with his cruel streak; Midir's cousin Conory, whose effeminate appearance masks a tough and steady nature; and many others, are all well drawn, interesting, and believable.

Most importantly, in *The Mark of the Horse Lord* a reader is made to understand and accept a moral imperative of an entirely different culture so that the self-sacrifice of Phaedrus at the end seems proper and, given his character development through the novel, inevitable. That alone would make this novel outstanding and, combined with its other strong qualities, makes it a fitting choice for the first Phoenix Award.

Life, Death, and Honor
in Rosemary Sutcliff's *Sun Horse, Moon Horse* and *Warrior Scarlet*

Mary Weichsel Ake

In honoring *The Mark of the Horse Lord* with the first Phoenix award, we have set the standard of excellence for all subsequent winners, for Rosemary Sutcliff is unquestionably the finest writer of historical novels for children and young adults. Awarded the 1959 Carnegie Medal for *The Lantern Bearers* and given the Order of the British Empire in 1975 for her contributions to children's literature, this painter-turned-author has created a body of work that will live in the memory of generations of children and adults.

Sutcliff's best work deals with the history of early Britain, in which she masterfully interweaves myth and saga with history. Her sense of time is marvelous. In her historical novels of early Britain, for example, time in the sense of months or years may be conveyed in a page or less, while several pages may detail an ancient ceremony. Yet the flow of the narrative is always even. What Sutcliff has done in her greatest books is to create for us a history alive with all the peoples (and always including the dark little original inhabitants) who came and conquered and intermixed over the generations that created Great Britain.

More than two thousand years ago, a tribe of horse herders called the Iceni lived on the chalk downs of England, where today there is an ancient carving known as the White Horse of Uffington. Many travelers come to admire this giant picture on the hillside made many years ago by the Iceni. Sutcliff's *Sun Horse, Moon Horse* tells how this carving might have been created. The Iceni were part of the early Iron Age. Their name means Horse People. In the story, Lubrin, third son of the tribal chieftain, has a gift for drawing. As he grows up, going through the rituals of the Boys' House following the Beltane fires of his ninth year and then, when sixteen, the ceremony of Man-Making, he hides this talent. When another group of horse people comes from the south and conquers Lubrin's tribe, killing his father and brothers and making slaves of those who survive, this talent for drawing sets the Iceni free again. One summer during their captivity, Lubrin bargains with Cradoc, their leader. He will create a white horse in honor of the Sun God for Cradoc's group, but it will also be for the Moon Goddess of Lubrin's people. If it meets with Cradoc's approval, Cradoc will set the Iceni free, along with horses and supplies, so they may go north to new herding lands told about in song.

To gain perspective for the gigantic chalk drawing, Lubrin climbs his favorite tree, his refuge from childhood days, and looks back across the valley at the chalk down. In his mind he pictures a white mare of flowing lines and full of life. He suddenly realizes it must be his own life's blood that will quicken the chalk horse. This is one of Sutcliff's strong themes, death and rebirth. It appears in many of her books. Boys must "die" to become men. A chief's blood must be the sacrifice for a new beginning.

The Iceni laboriously remove the sod and layers of chalk conforming to the lines marked on the turf by Lubrin. Slowly the shape of the white mare appears; Lubrin sees it is good. On Lammas Eve, both tribes are gathered on the hillside by the giant fires that have been lit in celebration. First, the herds of horses and cattle are driven between the flames. Then the remnants of the Iceni follow, for they, too, need the promise of fine offspring in their new northern home.

The next day, the Iceni set forth, but without Lubrin. Lubrin, body adorned with mystic symbols, joins Cradoc at the eye of the carved mare to fulfill the promise and his destiny. *Sun Horse, Moon Horse* is a short book, but a very powerful one, with its themes of life, death, rebirth, honor, and tradition, plus the mixing of different ancient peoples.

Warrior Scarlet is laid in the Bronze Age. It, too, is a powerful novel, beautifully written, of a boy named Drem who is determined to be a warrior despite the handicap of his withered arm. In this book, the ordeals, the tribulations that a young boy must struggle through while passing into manhood, this proving of worthiness, ties in with Sutcliff's concern for honor. *Warrior Scarlet* is a novel in which the reader becomes immersed in the story and its period as the rites and the rituals of the culture become real to the reader, just as does the daily life of the Bronze Age people. There is violence, but it is an integral part of the story, not there just for itself alone. The researched details of the time are so interwoven with the storytelling that one is unaware of them as such. Drem and his struggles within himself as he overcomes self-regard to reach his goal are one with the richly treated historical setting. Sutcliff is truly master of this type of novel, and her skill is never more evident than in *Warrior Scarlet*.

When Drem is twelve, he enters the Boys' House for training to become a warrior. Despite his withered arm, he is determined to prove himself worthy of the scarlet cloak by which warriors are identified. His best friend is the chieftain's son, Vortrix. The final test for each boy occurs at fifteen, when he must slay a wolf in single combat. One by one, the others achieve this feat (save one who is killed in the attempt). When Drem's turn comes, accompanied by the others in his group, he sets out to track down his prey. Unfortunately, he slips and misses the wolf. It attacks Drem, but is driven away by Vortrix, who cannot stand by and watch the death of his blood brother. As a result, Drem leaves his tribe and goes to live with the little dark people who herd sheep on the downs. Now an outcast, Drem slowly comes to terms with his fate. Although he is never quite reconciled to the loss of his goal to wear the scarlet of the warrior, he learns to accept his new responsibilities, and to do them well.

One cold winter's evening, the ancient sheepherder, Doli, does not return. Despite the fierce weather, in his concern over Doli, Drem leaves in search of him. Struggling through the blizzard, following a faint track, Drem reaches a cliff, where he finds that Doli has fallen over and is severely injured. Sending his sheepdog back for help, Drem prepares to protect Doli against the wolves that will most surely come. In a thrilling climactic fight, Drem kills a huge wolf just as the hunters, summoned by his dog, arrive. Vortrix is with them, and it is he who discovers that the wolf is the same one Drem had failed to kill during the Wolf Slaying.

Thus it is that Drem is allowed to return to his own people and undergo the final rites to become a man and a warrior. Rich in details of the ceremonies of the Bronze Age people and their daily life, Sutcliff's *Warrior Scarlet* has a fine plot as well in the maturing of Drem and the events of his tribal life. As with Lubrin of *Sun Horse, Moon Horse*, the themes of life, death, and honor come together for the making of a man.

Dawn Wind and *Knight's Fee:*
Two Medieval Novels by Rosemary Sutcliff

M. Sarah Smedman

In her essay "History Is People," Rosemary Sutcliff says that "the reading child is liable to absorb ideas from books which may remain with him for the rest of his life, and even play some part in determining the kind of person that he is going to become. I do try to put over to the child reading any book of mine some kind of ethic, a set of values beyond the colour-television-two-cars-in-the-garage variety" (Haviland 306). Though *Dawn Wind* and *Knight's Fee* are set at very different times, at opposite ends of medieval England, they convey similar values: bravery under duress, reliability, and loyalty to one's friends and one's principles.

Dawn Wind is set in sixth-century Britain at Aquae Sulis (Bath, as we know it). It covers twelve years in the life of Owain, who is, with the exception of the war hound Dog, the sole survivor of the battle at Aquae Sulis, the battle which killed his father and brother and severely wounded himself.

Unaware that the Saxons have destroyed his native land, Owain makes his way toward home, on the way collapsing on the doorstep of an elderly country couple, who nurse him back to health. Once well again, Owain is compelled to continue his quest to the burnt-out city of Vironconium, where he finds only one other living creature, a ragged waif named Regina. Planning to make their way together to Gaul, they start for the coast. When Regina falls ill, Owain carries her, eventually, into a Saxon settlement where he gives himself as a thrall in exchange for the nursing of Regina. A visitor to the village buys Owain for a piece of silver and takes him to Seals Island, repaying the boy's faithful service with trust and kindness. At first regarding the Saxons as enemies, Owain gradually feels the affinity between himself and them more strongly than his hatred. When Beornwulf, his master, is killed in battle, Owain, now freed, agrees to return to care for Beornwulf's family until the latter's hot-headed young son, Bryni, reaches fifteen. Then once again Owain agrees to extend his time for a year to save Lilla, one of Beornwulf's daughters, from marriage with a cruel, tyrannical older man, Vadir, a long-time enemy.

Throughout the novel good and evil are interlocked in physical and psychic battles. Good finally triumphs when Owen attempts to save his archenemy, Vadir, from being trampled by the great white horse, Teitri, at whose birthing both had assisted. Owain is gradually transformed from a boy driven only by the instinct for survival into a strong, noble young man who voluntarily postpones his own freedom to honor the request of a dying master. Owain's last act of mercy toward Vadir is his redemption: finally he is free to return to Regina.

Dawn Wind is so rich in language and symbol, in vivid creation of place that it is hardly justifiable to have to comment on it here so briefly. Perhaps as meaningful as any analysis of Sutcliff's power of language is the poetic response of one of my students to *Dawn Wind*: "If I were to think of one sound that best typifies this book," she wrote, "it would be that of a pulsing heart as the only sound in the world. That heart would beat, slow and steady, and be surrounded by silence in a world destroyed at the battle of Aquae Sulis. The Saxons have beaten the British, yet that one British heart continues to beat, and Owain crawls out of the rubble to become the protagonist who is symbolic of the British race. In his fight for survival amidst hunger and wounds and slavery and heartbreak, Owain becomes emblematic of the British spirit itself" (Rainey).

Like Owain, Randal, the protagonist of *Knight's Fee,* set in twelfth-century Britain, is also a child on his own, nine years old now, going on ten, and officially a dogboy:

> His name was Randal, Randal the Bastard, Randal the Thief. His father was a Breton Man-at-Arms, and his mother a Saxon lady. She, having nothing to live for, had died when he was born; his father had been killed when he was four years old, in the constant warfare along the Welsh Marches, and neither among his father's people nor his mother's was there any place for Randal. The only person who had ever shown him any kindness was Lovel the Huntsman, who had taken him over from the time when the woman who sold cheap wine to the men-at-arms had thrown him

out like an unwanted nestling because with his father dead there would be no more money for keeping him. Lovel had brought him up, or rather, allowed him to bring himself up in the kennels along with the hound puppies, and treated him as he treated all the rest of his charges, thrashing him mercilessly with the same long oxhide whip when he was wicked, purging him with buckthorn in the spring, and sitting up with him when he had the colic. (1)

In the story's initial incident, Randal, watching the arrival of the new Lord of Arundel Castle from the gatehouse roof, drops a fig he is eating on the nose of the lord's black stallion and thereby changes his whole life. Saved from the Lord's beating by Herluin the Minstrel, who wins the child in a chess game, Randal is given over to Sir Everard d'Aquillon to be raised with his grandson Bevis. The two boys eventually become great friends as together they are trained as squires. The plan is that Bevis will be knighted and Randal will remain his squire. However, here, as so often, the plans of men "gang aft aglay."

Knight's Fee is not only an absorbing story but an accurate account of the processes and rituals of knighthood. Before Bevis dies of wounds in the Battle of Tenchebrai, which ended Norman resistance to the English for years to come, he knights Randal, who inherits the stead of his friend and benefactor. *Knight's Fee,* because of its detailed and vivid depiction of place, its historical accuracy, and its immediacy, is much more than a formulaic Horatio Alger story in medieval costume. It is a sublime story of kinship, brotherhood, and friendship among human beings.

Several qualities common to both *Dawn Wind* and *Knight's Fee* stand out. First, the bond between the young characters begins in an episode in which both parties exhibit a sensitivity to and appreciation of nature. The incipient love between Owain and Regina is cemented by a blue tit which "sprang upward, hung for a moment on vibrating wings that were like tiny fans of blue green mist against the low sunlight" (61). Similarly, delight moves both Randal and Bevis when, running the hounds, their attention is caught

> by very beautiful little birds, and as they flittered from thistle head to thistle head, [the boys] saw the golden bars on their wings, and the patch of chestnut crimson on their foreheads. And then a gleam of sunlight woke under the apple trees—it was a grey, drifting day

of broken lights and shadows—and suddenly they were feathered jewels. (49-50)

The characters from both novels also understand the wisdom of silence in the presence of such natural beauty as birds, or the sea, or "one small white star [which] looked down at them through the charred beams and the bramble sprays, [and] which was somehow comforting" (*Dawn Wind* 82).

A second characteristic common to these novels is the close association of people—the cruel and wicked as well as the gentle and good—with animals, particularly dogs and horses. Scenes involving animals frequently anticipate and prefigure conflicts, even violent fights, among their owners, as the attack of the hounds upon the boar foreshadows the savage fight between Bryni and Vadir (*Dawn Wind* 257, 294).

Certain recurrent themes bind Sutcliff's novels together: the conflict between barbarism and humane civilization, between the forces of light and darkness; the capability of humans beings for sublime and loving self-sacrifice; and the recovery of mythic time, that sacred time when new beginnings are possible, through reenactment of mythic models and rituals.

All of Sutcliff's works attest to her mastery of language, not only, as already alluded to, in the particularizing of places so lovingly and unforgettably, but also in her talent for using the rhythms and figures of Old English in her recreation of the period's ethos. When Owain, for example, stands among the Saxon warriors welcoming St. Augustine to Kent, "it seemed to him that a glorious and shining thing was happening; he had a feeling of great wonder, and the shadows of the clouds over the marsh were the shadows of vast wings." But Owain's "winged moment" slips away, and he laughs ruefully. "The taste of one's own foolishness is just as sour [as the taste of sloes]. I thought this morning, just for a wingbeat of time, that—that something wonderful was happening. And all the while it was no more than a piece of statecraft being played out." Reminded by an elder that "even a piece of statecraft might hold your 'something wonderful' at its heart," Owain feels the "dawn wind stirring" (279, 289-90).

As real as Sutcliff's stories are, as immediate as she makes early British history, I as a reader do not participate in them as I do in most modern novels. I enter them in a different, a more reverent, way. And I come away from each awe-inspired, as if I too have witnessed a "glorious and shining thing" happening. Much of my response is due to the author's majestic use of language, which though it may occasionally turn purple, is often close to mystical. Sutcliff's novels are, for me, from start to finish novels of renewal; they depict what she explains in an afterword to *Knight's Fee* as the Old Faith of all Europe, which existed long before the Christian era but which coexisted with Christianity through the Middle Ages: "a God-King had to die every so often, and be born again in a new God-King, just as the year dies in the winter and is born again in the spring, and that only so could life go on" (240). In Sutcliff's novels, in the face of all odds, life does go on.

Works Cited

Haviland, Virginia, ed. *Children and Literature: Views and Reviews.* Glenview, Illinois: Scott, Foresman, 1973.

Rainey, Martha. "The Thematic Relationship of Character and Place in Rosemary Sutcliff's Historical Fiction." Unpublished paper for a graduate course in The Worlds of Juvenile Fiction. University of North Carolina—Charlotte, 1985.

Heroic Literature by Rosemary Sutcliff

Alethea Helbig

Among Rosemary Sutcliff's books are several retellings of heroic literature from oral tradition. Although at least one of her recent versions of the Arthur stories has received commendation, they and *Song for a Dark Queen,* the starkly dramatic account of the ill-used and fiercely determined Queen Boadicea of the British Iceni, are variously classed as fiction rather than old story. *Tristan and Iseult,* in Sutcliff's hands a tenderly told love story, seems to me curiously disjointed and lacking in impact. More skillfully and memorably retold, since they aptly catch the tenor of the originals and the spirit of their times, are *Beowulf* and *The Hound of Ulster.* Their highly pictorial, euphonious, vigorous style produces a strong storytelling quality that captures the occasional mischief, the dramatic conflict, and, in particular, the deep tragedy of these old stories.

The first published of these, *Beowulf,* concentrates upon the three major episodes of the great Anglo-Saxon epic: how Beowulf slays Grendel, then Grendel's mother, and then, after ruling for fifty years as King of the Geats, gives his life in slaying the fierce fire dragon that ravages his land. Sutcliff early establishes the sense of an actual storytelling situation with a little old sea captain narrator whose tale to the assembled Geats in their great hall hints of terrible and magnificent deeds to come. High in atmosphere, this initial scene sets the serious and somber note that persists throughout the book:

> And their Captain sat in the Guest Seat that faced the High Seat of the King, midway up the hall, and told the news of the coasts and islands and the northern seas.
>
> He leaned forward in the great carved seat, a small man with his hands on his knees, and his long-sighted seaman's gaze coming and going about the smoky hall, and told, among lesser matters,

> how Hrothgar, the great warrior king of the Danish folk, had built for himself a mighty mead-hall where he and his household warriors might feast and make merry, and give a fitting welcome to any strangers and wayfarers who came among them.
> "A great hall, a most fine hall!" said the Sea Captain, while the rest of his crew on the mead benches nodded and muttered their agreement. "Longer and loftier even than this in which my lord Hygelac has feasted us so royally tonight. And Hrothgar set up high on its gable end the gilded antlers of a stag, and called the place for that reason, Herorot the Hart. Aye, but he might have done better to have lived out his days in a shepherd's bothie; for small joy has the Danish King of his mead-hall." And he drank deep from the mead horn as it was handed to him, and shook his head, and waited to be asked why. (8-9)

And we, like the listeners of yore, also wait to be told why.

Appeal to sight, as well as to ear, continues, in passages keen with descriptive language:

> [Grendel] heard the laughter and the harp-song from the King's high hall, and it troubled him in his dark dreams, and he roused and came up out of the waste lands and snuffed about the porch. (10)

And in action scenes:

> Grendel prowled in, hating all men and all joy, and hungry for human life. So swift was his attack that no man heard an outcry; but when the dawn came, thirty of Hrothgar's best and noblest thanes were missing, and only the blood splashed on walls and floors, and the monster's footprints oozing red, remained to tell their fate. (11)

The theme is struck: clearly this is no commonplace monster, no ordinary evil that Beowulf, valiant hero, goes to face.

One continues to sense the storytelling situation through the occasionally harsh, at other times gently melodious diction and the carefully patterned phrases that portray, repeat, ebb and flow like a voice set to the accompaniment of deeper harp string, eloquently employing alliteration and kenning-like language to catch the spirit and poetic grandeur of the original:

> Then they set the four slow yoke of oxen straining up the steep slope to the headland, where the pyre stood waiting against the sky. They laid the body of Beowulf on the stacked brushwood and thrust in the torches, and presently all men far and wide saw the red fire on the Whale's Ness, and knew that Beowulf had gone to join his kindred.
> All night long the fire burned, and when it sank at dawn they piled about the ashes the precious things of the dragon's hoard, and upreared the golden banner over all. Then they set themselves to raise the barrow as the old King had bidden them . . . on the tenth day the great howe of piled stones stood finished, notching the sky for all time on the uttermost height of the Whale's Ness, where the cliffs plunged sheer to the sea.
> Then twelve chieftains of his bodyguard rode sunwise about it, singing the death song that the harpers had made for him. And when the song was sung, all men went away, and left Beowulf's barrow alone with the sea wind and the wheeling gulls and the distant ships that passed on the Sail-Road. (107-108)

The story ends, as it began, on a brooding note.

Sutcliff herself speaks as poet, bard, teller of high and far off tales to begin *The Hound of Ulster*, another story rich in epic and tragic values, addressing the reader directly: "This is the story of Cuchulain the Champion of Ulster, the greatest of all the heroes of the Red Branch. Listen, now" (9). Setenta, son of a mortal maiden and Lugh, the god of the sun, earns his hero name of Cuchulain when he kills a monster guard dog with his bare hands while yet a boy. He performs thereafter valorous deeds against Ulster's foes, struggling against both men and magic, and still young, perishes nobly, overwhelmed by hordes of enemies while defending his people, a death whose poignancy is rivaled in heroic literature only by that of Roland of French story.

Pictures abound, sharp with color and other imagery, as Sutcliff pulls together to form a unified story the disparate narratives that revolve around the hero and his friends and foes. His bride-to-be, the beautiful, assertive, and self-assured Emer, daughter of the Wily Forgall, is dark-haired almost as himself, and her skin white as mare's milk, and her eyes wide and proud and brilliant like the eyes of Fedelma, his favorite falcon. Her gown was green, dark as the leaves of the hill juniper, and balls of red gold hung at the ends of her long braids and swung a little as she moved among the warrior benches to keep the mead cups filled. (25)

Figures rich in suggestive language adorn the description of Cuchulain himself as he rides to court her:

"A small man—a boy—no, a man, dark and sad but best to look upon of all the men of Ireland. He wears a crimson cloak clasped at the shoulder with a brooch of gold, and it flies from him like a flame in the wind of his going, and on his back is a crimson shield with a silver rim worked over with golden figures of beasts."(27)

This passage not only is vivid with descriptive detail that evokes the sense of a long-gone time and its nobility but also hints of the darkness that lies ahead for the hero.

Supernatural aspects lend to the story a dimension that is absent from the more realistic *Beowulf*. In battle, a characteristic frenzy seizes Cuchulain, which over the years becomes a

thing that all men knew and trembled at; and the way of it was this: from head to heel he quivered like a bullrush in a running stream, and the muscles of his neck stood out like the coils of a writhing serpent. One eye sank deep into his head, and the other thrust out, full of flames, and foam burst from his mouth like the fleece of a three-year-old ram and his heartbeat sounded like the roars of a lion as he rushes on his prey. A light blazed upon his forehead, and his hair grew tangled as the branches of a thorn bush. And from the crown of his head sprang a jet of dark blood that shot tree-high towards the sky and spread into a rolling murk that cast its shadow all about him. (59-60)

Cuchulain slays his own only son, not knowing who the youth who challenges him is, for a particularly heart-rending episode, defeats a valiant woman warrior, Aifa, in one filled with much direct action and conflict, wins Emer in a humorous passage, also action-filled, while irony characterizes the scene of Bricrieu's Feast and sweet and sad romance that of Deirdre and the sons of Usna. With all this variety, the storytelling remains rich in the lilt and cadence we associate with old Ireland. Says Cathbad the Druid, his seer power come upon him,

> "The boy who takes up the spear and shield of manhood on this day will become the greatest and most renowned of all the warriors of Ireland, men will follow at his call to the world's end, and his enemies will shudder at the thunder of his chariot wheels, and the harpers shall sing of him while green Ireland yet rises above the sea; but his flowering-time shall be brief as that of the white bell-bine, opening in the morning and drooping before night. For he shall not live to count one grey hair at his temples...."(20)

The strong storytelling voice relieves the melodrama at the romantic, sorrowful, yet intensely heroic conclusion:

> So Conall laid ... [Emer and Cuchulain] in the same grave, and raised one pillar stone over them, and carved their names upon it in the Ogham script. And all Ulster wept for their loss: because of the story of Cuchulain the Hound of Ulster, there was no more. No more. (192)

Sutcliff's muse, if sometimes fulsome, is appropriate for Cuchulain's tale.

Famed storyteller Ruth Sawyer said good storymaking should create pictures in the hearers' minds and by scenes and sounds carry the listeners back to yesteryear and give them the flavor and feel of the times and happenings that once were (Sawyer in a recording). If Sawyer is right, and that constitutes good storytelling, then Sutcliff's is good storytelling indeed, for that is precisely what she does in these books, and superbly so. She carries the listener and reader back to the times that once were.

Work Cited

Sawyer, Ruth. "Ruth Sawyer Comments About Storytelling." *Ruth Sawyer, Storyteller.* Weston, Conn.: Weston Woods, n. d.

The 1986 Phoenix Award Winner

Queenie Peavy

Robert Burch

Georgia schoolgirl Queenie Peavy, 13, proudly sports a chip on her shoulder. Her anti-social escapades in and out of school compound the problems of poverty and a father in prison. Threatened with reform school, acknowledging misplaced filial loyalty, Queenie comes to see that life can be good if she takes responsibility for making it so. Skillfully realized characters, a strong sense of life during the Depression, judicious use of humor, and a modest, unassuming style create a distinctive and memorable girl's growing-up story.*

---

*This and the following papers about the 1986 Phoenix Award winner were previously published in the *Proceedings of the Thirteenth Annual Conference of the Children's Literature Association,* ed. Susan R. Gannon and Ruth Anne Thompson. The Children's Literature Association, 1988.

Acceptance: 1986 Phoenix Award

Robert Burch

Thank you very much. I'm grateful to all of you for this award and am deeply honored. In our age of disposable wares, including books that are timely one day and old-hat the next, anyone writing in the children's field is fortunate to have a book that "hangs in there," as it were, for any real length of time, but to have it win an award from so distinguished a group as yours is very special indeed.

And I'm delighted to have this opportunity to be with you again. After the Charlotte conference, I felt that I had a number of new friends. By now, I consider you *old friends*. And, for giving me this splendid award, you are certainly my *good friends*.

Did you know that the Phoenix is the symbol of Atlanta—which is home territory for me? I live in a country town just south of it. Of course, it wasn't until after Sherman burned down Atlanta that we needed this appropriate symbol! But the Phoenix has served as a reminder to all Georgians over the years that it is possible to rebuild from ashes. The Phoenix that you've given me will serve as a reminder that it's possible to produce work that lasts—twenty years, at least. Of course, a true phoenix, according to most of the Greek writers, lasted five hundred years or longer, but I'm glad you settled on *twenty* for the award. Incidentally, when I bragged to friends that I was to receive it, several of them said, in effect, "Isn't that a neat award?" The idea of recognizing something nowadays that isn't brand new seemed somehow revolutionary, and they felt that the members of The Children's Literature Association must be very astute and highly discerning people to have created the award. I explained to them that you were very astute and highly discerning in giving it to *Queenie Peavy!*

That isn't really the way I feel. There are many other books deserving of this year's award, which makes me especially pleased that *Queenie Peavy* was chosen.

I have to admit that I started writing the book for the wrong reason. After I'd written several of my earlier stories, a writer friend in New York dismissed them as *un*creative efforts: "They're purely autobiographical," she insisted. "All those yarns about ragged-ass boys growing up during the Great Depression."

I asked what I needed to do to prove that I was what she called a *real writer*, and she said, "Use a girl for a central character. Then I'll know it isn't your life story."

I don't know now why it seemed important to convince her of anything—probably the motivation was less than honorable—but I started the story just to show her that I could write it. Of course, somewhere along the line I became genuinely concerned about Queenie.

When I visited with you in '84 your conference theme was "Pride of Place: Wellspring for Story," which I like very much as it summed up thoughts I'd been trying to put together about the rural South as inspiration for writing. This year's theme, "From Hannibal to Oz: Journeys in Children's Literature," appeals to me also, as journeys of any sort have always interested me.

Queenie Peavy's "journey" was, without her realizing it—perhaps without my realizing it—an inward quest of the mind and spirit. At first, she's in a blind alley because of the fierce loyalty to her father and her need to believe that he cares about her. When she faces the truth as it is instead of as she wishes it to be, she heads in the right direction. In a final scene, when she deliberately tosses away the stone instead of aiming it, I hope that young readers are convinced that she has chosen the positive route and will stay on it.

Incidentally, my working title for the book had been *A Stone's Throw* as Queenie was literally a crack shot with a stone. Also, she was within a stone's throw of leading a decent life if she'd learn to behave herself. Annis Duff, my editor at the time, suggested giving the book a different name.

To some extent, I've overdone character names in titles, although in that instance I'm glad it was used. But I almost always have title trouble. That's one reason I'm so impressed by the ones of you who not only plan your conferences but come up with themes for them that are interesting and provocative.

I've never started a story without first giving it a title. The problem has been that frequently the story I write bears little resemblance to the story I'd planned. I have a new book that's scheduled for publication in October, and my working title for it was *The Poet Laureate of the Sixth Grade at Stokes Elementary School in Flag City, Georgia*. In addition to sounding as if E. L. Konigsburg had helped me with it, it was, of course, much too long. So I shortened it to *The Poet Laureate of the Sixth Grade*, but later changed that—for two reasons: 1) elementary students probably don't know what a poet laureate is, and 2) they may not *want to know* what a poet laureate is! So the title—already on the dust jacket and too late change again—is *King Kong and Other Poets*. King Kong is the pseudonym of one of the students in a poetry-writing contest.

I thought of bringing a couple of pages of manuscript to read while I have a captive audience, but instead, I'll read one of the children's poems. It's written by a kid who chose as his pen name, Alexander the Great, Military Conqueror and King of Macedonia. His pseudonym indicates that at least he's been paying attention in social studies. The poem goes like this:

> Once I took a river ride
>   With my brother and his bride.
> It was just before their wedding day
>   Which is over now, and they're home to stay.
>
> When they got back from their honeymoon
>   They moved in with us and took over my room.
> If we go on the river for another ride
>   I wish that I could drown the bride.

No doubt, you'll be relieved to know that he doesn't win the contest. There's a girl in the class, however—a mousy-looking new kid—who exhibits, if not special talent, at least enthusiasm for writing poetry.

Because all the other children have written about their own lives, they assume that her poems are from firsthand experience also, and are envious when she writes of her privileged life, her loving family, and a collection of exotic pets and expensive toys. They don't understand poetic license, and she's able to use her poetry as a vehicle for acceptance, even though acceptance at first is based on misconception. Later, when she realizes that the friendship is real, her life begins to change.

I wanted to write a story about someone who doesn't fit in, and I enjoyed working with themes of special meaning to me: reality and dreams, indirect and intentional deception, poverty and wealth, and the age-old questions of "Who am I?" and "On what basis will I be accepted?"

In a sense, her story is a journey. It's a journey toward the discovery of the power of friendship, which, to me, is one of the most pleasant and meaningful journeys any of us take in life. And that brings me back to where I started—our being friends, you and me, and the pleasure it is to be with you.

Thank you again for the Phoenix Award.

Robert Burch

Modesty, understatement, and quiet humor are qualities that wear well. They are characteristic of the books of Robert Burch, author of realistic stories mostly set in the rural South, many of them in the 1930s when he was a child.

Burch was born in Inman, Georgia, in 1925. He was graduated from the University of Georgia with a major in agriculture, served in the army in New Guinea and Australia during World War II, and has made his home in Fayetteville, Georgia. After the war, in a course at Hunter College, New York, taught by Dr. William Lipkind, Burch started writing for children. His first couple of books, both for young children, are conventional and slightly didactic, but with *Tyler, Wilkin, and Skee* he found his true voice. This episodic story of three brothers living on a Georgia farm during the Great Depression rings true, with everyday hardships, disappointments, and triumphs. Even Christmas, not likely to offer anything except new overalls, has its joys: they get a puppy from a neighbor, pool their money to buy their father a flashlight only to find that he has bought one for the family, and agree that their "cup runneth over."

Family love, or the lack of it as in *Queenie Peavy* and with the orphan Skinny, is at the root of most of Burch's novels. D.J.'s stubborn refusal to cooperate alienates him from his family until his pesty little brother, Renfroe, almost dies; in *Simon and the Game of Chance* the children struggle to keep the family going while their mother is in a mental hospital; in the Ida Early books an eccentric housekeeper becomes a surrogate mother for the four Sutton children, replacing rigid Aunt Earnestine. Burch's families are not perfect, but the value of a loving home life is treated seriously, and its lack creates the major problems of several of his stories.

Burch's books have received meaningful honors. He was named Georgia Author of the Year for *Joey's Cat*. *Queenie Peavy* won the Jane Addams Peace Association Children's Book Award, the Child Study Children's Book Committee at Bank Street College Award, and the

George G. Stone Center for Children's Books Recognition of Merit Award, and was named to the *Choice* magazine list of suggested children's books for an academic library and *The Horn Book Magazine* Fanfare list. *Ida Early Comes Over the Mountain* was an honor book for the *Boston Globe-Horn Book* Fiction Award. Two of his earlier books have been reissued by the University of Georgia Press.

Like their author, Burch's books are inclined to be quiet and unsensational, dealing with basic themes in an unpretentious way. His characters are memorable, developed to seem like real people, and his stories evoke emotion without sentimentality. The Phoenix Award attests to the lasting appeal of these qualities.

Books by Robert Burch

The Traveling Bird. Illus. Susanne Suba. New York: McDowell Obolensky, 1959.
A Funny Place to Live. Illus. W. R. Lohse. New York: Viking, 1962.
Tyler, Wilkin, and Skee. Illus. Don Sibley. New York: Viking, 1963; Athens: University of Georgia, 1990.
Skinny. Illus. Don Sibley. New York: Viking, 1965; Athens: University of Georgia, 1990.
D. J.'s Worst Enemy. Illus. Emil Weiss. New York: Viking, 1965.
Queenie Peavy. Illus. Jerry Lazare. New York: Viking, 1966; Dell Yearling, 1975; Puffin, 1987.
Renfroe's Christmas. Illus. Rocco Negri. New York: Viking, 1968.
Joey's Cat. Illus. Don Freeman. New York: Viking, 1969.
Simon and the Game of Chance. Illus. Fermin Rocker. New York: Viking, 1970.
The Hunting Trip. Illus. Susanne Suba. New York: Scribner, 1971.
Doodle and the Go-Cart. Illus. Alan Tiegreen. New York: Viking, 1972.
Hut School and the Wartime Home-Front Heroes. Illus. Ronald Himler. New York: Viking, 1974.
The Jolly Witch. Illus. Leigh Grant. New York: Dutton, 1975.
Two That Were Tough. Illus. Richard Cuffari. New York: Viking, 1976.
The Whitman Kick. New York: Dutton, 1977.
Wilkin's Ghost. Illus. Lloyd Bloom. New York: Viking, 1978.
Ida Early Comes over the Mountain. New York: Viking, 1980.
Christmas with Ida Early. New York: Viking, 1983.
King Kong and Other Poets. New York: Viking, 1986.

Three Problem Novels that Hold Up

Rebecca Lukens

Our Phoenix prize-winner, *Queenie Peavy*, stands as an example of what we hoped to see in the run of problem novels of the 1960s and early 70s. But, as book after book appeared, we were often disappointed, for little of the fiction that followed measured up to *Queenie*, for a variety of reasons. First of all, few had Burch's skill in characterization, not only of protagonist but also of minor characters, followed by his development of significant themes relevant not only to childhood but to all human beings. In addition, he successfully evokes setting, gives the flavor of Southern dialogue, and all with subtle humor.

Looking quickly at the novel, we meet Queenie on page one, chapter one, called "Deadly Aim":

> Queenie Peavy was the only girl in Cotton Junction who could chew tobacco. She could also spit it—and with deadly aim. She could do a number of things with a considerable degree of accuracy, most of them unworthy of her attention.

Immediately Queenie is not only interesting, but surely atypical, clearly defiant, no doubt troublesome, perhaps even delinquent. We follow her as she chews and spits tobacco, throws rocks with absolute accuracy, challenges the boys in her class at almost anything, arranges the downed sapling so that nasty, taunting Cravey Mason falls into the creek—and is simultaneously the best student in the class. She does what we would have liked to do: Queenie is the perfect combination of personal achievement and the universal wish to rebel against conforming and to be oneself, to jump out of the bushes and scare smaller children and yet be beloved by them. Most certainly, she represents a universal wish to retaliate against those who taunt us, sneer at our families, or denigrate us in any way. She has the courage to go alone to see the judge, even though she is afraid he will send her off to the reformatory. She holds her head up when she hears cries of "Queenie's daddy's in the chain gang!" and eagerly awaits her father's return on parole (17). Queenie is proud, competent, and loyal—traits we admire and wish for ourselves.

Involved in Queenie's struggles, we root for her and fear for her; what's more, we explain her to her teachers, apologize for her to the principal, advise her about her defiant behavior, and earnestly hope she will be strong enough to control her actions. We know long before Queenie does what the themes of the novel are. She tells Ol' Domnick the rooster, deceiver of his hens, "They don't know when you're lying and when you're not!" (111), and we mutter, "Queenie, listen to yourself." Queenie, thinking about how her father is violating his parole, admits to herself that she had known "all the time, and refused to face up to it, that he had brought on his own troubles" (143). Again we mutter, "Queenie, you're talking about yourself." As she faces the one remaining window in the church tower and raises her throwing arm, she says to herself, "But who are you hurting in the long run?" (155), this time we mutter, "Right, Queenie. You must know whom you're hurting."

Robert Burch has created a believable, memorable character, made us care and kept us in suspense about her, and brought the internal conflict to a most satisfactory close. While we have anxiously cheered the recalcitrant Queenie, we know she has made some essential discoveries. We applaud her for her strength to change.

Equally successful in depiction of the internal struggle to face up to what our actions are doing to ourselves and others is *D.J.'s Worst Enemy*. Here Burch uses first person narrative to follow D. J. through his summer on the Georgia farm, his stubborn refusal to cooperate or be part of any group, including his family, that causes him all kinds of trouble. The simple recreations of rural children during the Depression seem to us idyllic, as we get into wayward mischief: frightening others by imitating a raging bull, seeking a no-reason-all-out-brawl with Monroe and Britt, riding on the mule-powered wagon and dropping off to run behind, watching bully Ratty Logan get beaten up for a change—all this with D. J. constantly looking for a way either to start something or to get back at someone who, he maintains, started it first.

Three Problem Novels that Hold Up

Again we are caught up in skillful characterization, this time not only with the central character, D. J., but also with proper Clara May and Skinny Little Renfroe, the five-year-old brother. To D. J., Skinny Little Renfroe is a pest to be pestered. Pa "lectures" D. J. about being his own worst enemy and suggests that he try becoming a part of the family. D. J.'s internal struggle involves controlling his impulses to lie a little, deceive a little, trip someone up, if just a bit. And this is what gets him into trouble, for he pegs a corncob at Renfroe resulting in a slight wound that brings on blood poisoning and Renfroe's long, nearly fatal stay in the hospital. By the time Renfroe returns, D. J. has worked a good bit more mischief, but his joy in Renfroe's recovery makes him "join the family again."

The flavor in Burch's writing is a flavor of the rural South: phrases like D. J.'s "getting the urge to be grown" at the square dance; being "out-of-the-grass" or through planting; "laying-by" or waiting for harvest; "chunking the fire under the washpots." Not only does Burch capture flavor in dialogue, but also the Depression setting, with the mule-drawn wagon, the mail order radio with a cord and plug, useless in the farmhouse without electricity, the swim in the mill pond, the barefoot summers and the need to save for "school duds," the village doctor who owns a rare Model A Ford. All these details evoke for us the time and place Burch seems to know so well.

In 1968, Viking published *Renfroe's Christmas*, starring this time D. J.'s little brother, Renfroe. Once again Burch evokes a time, a place, and the Madison family. Renfroe and Clara May sing to the cows, hoping they will yield more milk if entertained and contented. It is Christmas time. Although sister Clara May professes to think it is more blessed to give than to receive, and suggests to Renfroe that it is possible to overcome selfishness, Renfroe is, thank heaven, normal. The brief story of fifty-nine pages calls up the simplicity and excitement of preparation for church Christmas pageants, and the chaos and unpredictability of the program itself. Joy in simple things pervades the story. Christmas brings Renfroe three small gifts, a lasso, a yoyo, and a Mickey Mouse watch, "the finest thing [he's] ever owned by himself."

Once again Burch presents an internal conflict to be resolved, this time between Renfroe's wish to keep his precious gifts and the feeling of how rich he is in comparison to others. Here Burch again, thank goodness, avoids an unrealistically generous Renfroe; the boy does not give away his lasso nor his yoyo. Renfroe just struggles with the "oughts." But when Crazy Nathan, about to go away to a special school, holds the watch, admires it silently, and smiles—the first time Renfroe has seen such a smile—Renfroe first walks away with a feeling of surprise and pleasure. Then he turns, gives the watch to Crazy Nathan, saying that he will have more time to admire it than Renfroe will, and walks slowly away. But he wonders if he shouldn't turn around again and suggest that, yes, Crazy Nathan ought to give it back. Thus, we like Renfroe even more. He's reluctant, not unreal, good, but honestly struggling with selfishness.

The wonderful thing about reading several Robert Burch books in a row is that they are all so thoroughly of-a-piece. We appreciate these characters more each time we read about them. Mischief, imagination, the simple life lived with complex emotions, and the struggle to deal with the most ordinary and credible imperfections—these are the stuff of which the fine novels for any age can be made. There need not be breath-holding suspense, shattering climax, nothing sensational or sentimental, but just children whose anxieties and mischief-making are our own impulses made visible. The stories are good stories, in their interest and in their values. Robert Burch holds up well under careful scrutiny.

Robert Burch's Forte: Books Laid in Rural Georgia

Mary Weichsel Ake

Robert Burch is part of Georgia. He was born, raised, and educated in that state and now lives there. His love for the rural Georgia of his youth appears in most of his books for children, which are realistically remembered, lived experiences. The events that take place in them may seem grim, but they nevertheless carry the conviction of truth. They tell about things that could happen to real people, the everyday events of living, the crises of life. Burch has said, "And I cannot imagine a theme in a children's story strong enough to hold anything together that does not, in the final analysis, turn out to be moral, or at least morally sound. Stronger stories in every sense are likely to result when the writer is free to tackle whatever is meaningful to him" (Burch 263).

His first work, *The Traveling Bird,* reminds me of the later Shel Silverstein book, *The Giving Tree.* Or rather the reverse, I suppose. In this case, it is not a tree but a bird—a very special, wise bird that sets out to help a young boy realize his heart's desire. The parakeet is given to the boy, who really wants a puppy. The bird tries to help the child by locating a puppy lost in a storm and guiding the boy through the somewhat dangerous rescue. Then, alas, the true owner of the dog comes to claim it. During the first part of the story, the boy does not really care much for the bird. In fact, he resents the creature, because he still wants a puppy. Despite the bird's best efforts to win the boy's friendship, it simply doesn't work out. One day the bird takes the child to a pet store and tells him to choose any dog in the shop. Ecstatic, the boy returns home with a new puppy, so joyful he forgets even to thank the bird. When the next morning the boy returns to the pet store for the bird, he finds it gone. The pet store owner explains that the bird had arranged to be exchanged for a puppy, sacrificing himself that the boy might find joy. In tears, the boy runs away, leaving behind the puppy that had followed him to the shop. Then, realizing the generosity of the bird and his own responsibility to both bird and dog, he goes back and gets the puppy, intending to care properly for it.

The writing is uneven, and the story is preachy. However, Burch's skill at touching the emotions is evident already in this first book, and, in retrospect, his present narrative style is recognizable in its beginnings.

The quite different *A Funny Place to Live*, Burch's next published title, is aimed at very young children. The theme is that everything has its proper home. Two children lost in a forest meet with various animals and birds whose homes, of course, are not appropriate for the humans. Finally the two are guided by an owl to their own house in a forest clearing. The children are happy to be home, but the animals think the children's dwelling is a "funny place to live." Like his first book, this, too, is didactic, a concept book intended to entertain and at the same time to show different kinds of habitats. Like his first book, this, too, heralds better writing and more imaginative stories to come.

The episodic *Tyler, Wilkin, and Skee* introduces us to the setting of Burch's best works: rural Georgia. It concerns three close brothers during the Depression and deals with the farm life Burch knows well through his own experiences. Its events rise out of memories of his youth, and its force from his ability to recreate them clearly and memorably for us and link them to our own lives at the same time. Malcom Usrey puts it well: "Although Robert Burch has used a regional setting, he universalizes the action, characters, and themes of his fiction. His novels speak elemental truths: wealth does not necessarily create happiness; material progress does not change the basic needs of people; rural life and the land are important to any nation; poverty is not always degrading; and family and community, good or bad, are usually what people make them" (203).

Each chapter in *Tyler, Wilkin, and Skee* tells a separate story about a year's mostly everyday happenings. But some episodes relate special occurrences. The brothers enjoy riding in the neighbor's automobile, a rare treat. When they are promised a ride to the county fair in September, they are elated and look forward to the occasion with eager anticipation. But when the car comes by, it is filled with relatives of the neighbor and there is room for only one of the Coley boys. Though sadly, they decline the ride, sticking together then—as in all things important. The next August, however, all win a trip with their 4-H project. The book exudes gentle humor, the warmth of a loving family, simple living (the not-rich-but-never-got-poor feeling is strong), and of neighbor helping neighbor. This book stands as a worthy forerunner of Burch's later highly successful novels like *Skinny* and *Queenie Peavy*.

The protagonist of *Skinny* is appropriately nicknamed. A puny, bony, sturdy kid, he even manages to joke about his physique, revealing the attitude that enables him to cope with the hard life he is forced to lead. An orphan, he lives and works for his keep in the hotel owned by kind, warm Miss Bessie. It is summer in the small town, and the big events are the carnival and the watermelon festival. Skinny is cheerful, friendly, helpful, honest, and illiterate. He sets tables, waits on customers, clears away, taking an earnest pride in the place. Sunday School provides his only peer companionship. Otherwise, his friends are the adults with whom he rooms at the hotel. Miss Bessie would like to adopt him, but can't, being a single lady. When a construction man comes to stay at the hotel and he and Miss Bessie become good friends, Skinny's hopes rise. But his dream is not to come true, since the construction man has an itchy foot, and Skinny ends up in a church orphanage forty miles away. Although he could take his dog, RFD, along, he leaves him with Miss Bessie. Skinny has come to love her and doesn't want her to be lonely without him.

The book excels in characterization. It is easy to identify with Skinny; his problems become ours. The characters seem real and believable. A warm feeling of caring and respect for just plain people pervades the story and underscores Burch's excellent storytelling.

Works Cited

Burch, Robert. "The New Realism." *The Horn Book Magazine*, 47 (1971): 257-264.

Usrey, Malcolm. "Robert Burch." *Twentieth Century Children's Writers*. New York: St. Martin's, 1978.

Family Harmony and Love of Life in Four Books by Robert Burch

M. Sarah Smedman

The four books which are the focus of my presentation are representative of the range and the quality of Robert Burch's work. Two, *Joey's Cat* and *The Hunting Trip,* appear in picture book form; the other two, *Simon and the Game of Chance* and *Doodle and the Go-Cart,* are novels for the intermediate reader.

In 1970, Burch was named Georgia Author of the Year for *Joey's Cat,* a warm story of a small boy who worries and watches over his Mama Cat's kittens as best he can from below their box-nest "high on a pile of crates in the garage." When Mama Cat, who is quite capable of chasing off dogs and other cats who menace her brood, is so disturbed that she moves a kitten into the house, Joey knows she needs help in protecting her litter. Father helps him trap a predator possum, Mama allows the feline family to share her home, and Joey and his cat exchange knowing winks. In understated prose, Burch captures the feelings of a child for his pet and conveys the intimacy among disparate personalities in a family, a dominant theme in all the books which fall to my province to examine. Because of the story's insight into the experience and emotions of a child, it seems as fresh today as when it was published.

Simon and the Game of Chance is a story that will appeal not only to intermediate readers but to grown-ups as well. A refreshing antidote, or balance, to contemporary portrayals of sibling rivalry, the story depicts five brothers and a sister holding together their home with their upright, but stern, father while their mother is in a sanitarium recuperating from depression and "withdrawn" after the birth and death of her seventh baby, a second daughter. The outstanding quality of *Simon and the Game of Chance* is its sensitive portrayal of a web of relationships in a comparatively short novel. The book focuses on thirteen-year-old Simon, who is too young to be one of the older boys and too old to be one of the younger boys and whose sense of humor and athletic prowess fail to impress his serious, no-nonsense father.

With his mother in the hospital, Simon becomes more dependent on his nineteen-year-old sister, with whom he has always been close. When Clarissa falls in love and is about to be married, Simon is so lonely and scared that, rather than telling Clarissa how much he will miss her, he says he hopes something will occur to prevent the wedding. Something does.

The groom-to-be is killed in the explosion of a barbershop furnace. In her grief Clarissa becomes almost as withdrawn as their mother had been, and Simon's anxiety couples itself with his guilt to make his life almost insupportable. It is their father's insight, firmness, and gradually more demonstrative affection that leads Clarissa back into the center of the family.

Weaving in and out of Simon's relationships with his sister and father are those with his older and younger brothers and his teammates; those of his siblings with their father, friends and each other; those of Aunt Rainey with her brother and his children; Clarissa's with her fiance. Underlying them all is Mrs. Bradley's with her husband and children. Although she is away except at the beginning and end of the story, Mrs. Bradley, the mother, is very much a presence throughout. By the end, Simon has learned that life, like a game of chance, holds a lot of happiness as well as sadness.

Not as complex a book as *Simon, Doodle and the Go-Cart* exudes its author's love for the Georgia countryside he calls home. From what Bob Burch has said about his childhood, I suspect that much of Doodle Rounds' story is autobiographical. Certainly Burch, unlike Doodle, was not an only child. He may or may not have had so burning a desire for a go-cart (or some other mechanized vehicle) that it motivated him to make extraordinarily individualized and personable scarecrows, train himself to be a fishing guide, or become a winter trapper. But assuredly he knows the small towns, the farmland, the river and its path so vividly recreated in the book. And I have no doubt that he must have been as close friends with the farm animals as Doodle is with Godfrey, the calf with which he races, and with Addie Flowers, the mule which helps him think, watches his races as placid spectator, and always urges him on.

This book not only captures the comfortable mutual concerns and friendship among Doodle and his parents but also evinces the author's keen observation of the humorous foibles of town and country folk. While Burch is not nearly as garrulous as Garrison Keillor, his sensitivity to and appreciation of these people are just as winsome, people like Doodle's cousin Glenn Carter, who doesn't covet a go-cart but gets one for Christmas anyway; Aunt Peggy Carter who, expecting important town society guests, can hardly wait to get rid of the Rounds family during the Christmas duty visit; and the big kid, Butch Proctor, who never misses an opportunity to make fun of Doodle's abortive efforts to earn the $210 necessary to achieve his dreams.

Doodle's treasures are the go-cart he dreams of owning from the moment he rides one at a classmate's party and Addie Flowers the mule. At the end of the story Doodle decides to forego the go-cart rather than sell Addie. The bed-rock values upon which the novel is constructed—loyalty, patience, perseverance, and staying "in tune with nature"—prevail over selfishness, seizing the easiest way, and materialism.

"Crisp and clear," said the man, "a perfect day for hunting!"

So begins *The Hunting Trip*, a gentle, humorous book, again of the wonders of nature and of peace, the peace which begins at home. In the rhythms and tone of the folktale, the man with his very young wife go hunting with their hounds. Each time they flush game, the very young wife—the innocent child—suggests a reason why the grass finches, the ducks, the squirrels, the deer should live. At dusk, the couple goes home, the wife to milk the cow and gather the eggs, the man—not wanting to waste bullets (a refrain in the story)—to the store to trade them for peanut butter and jam to go with the eggs. After dinner, the very young wife toasts her feet (always cold when it comes to shooting wildlife) before the fire and revels in the fun of hunting. Innocence has rid this tiny world of injustice.

The Hunting Trip epitomizes in folksy prose the themes of family harmony, joy in the world and in life, themes which have been the heartbeat of these four satisfying, well-told stories.

Four Mid-Seventies Books by Robert Burch

Mark I. West

The four books that Robert Burch wrote during the mid-1970s vary considerably in content and quality. Two of these books, *Hut School and the Wartime Home-Front Heroes* and *The Whitman Kick*, fit neatly within the pattern that Burch had established in the 1960s. Like his earlier children's books, these two are set in small-town Georgia during the 1930s and '40s and feature children or teenagers as the main characters. The other two books, however, *The Jolly Witch* and *Two That Were Tough,* differ significantly from his earlier works. In *The Jolly Witch* Burch tries his hand at writing a fantasy, and in *Two That Were Tough* he turns his attention to the concerns of the elderly. In fact, though this story is intended for young readers, children play only minor roles in the book. Although all four are worth reading, *The Whitman Kick* and *Two That Were Tough* outshine these other two shelf-mates.

As its title suggests, *Hut School and the Wartime Home-Front Heroes* focuses on childhood during a time of war. The story takes place two years after America entered World War II. Kate Coleman, the book's central character, initially thinks of war as an inconvenience and an adventure but not as a tragedy. She misses the family outings that the fuel shortage has brought to an end, but she enjoys working in the victory garden with her father. Kate has similar feelings of ambivalence when her sixth-grade class is temporarily relocated to a cabin due to overcrowded conditions at her school. She is disappointed in the cabin's Spartan furnishings, but she likes walking through the cow pasture on her way to the lunchroom.

Although many of the chapters deal with her experiences at school, the war theme is always present. By the end of the book, Kate begins to realize what a terrible thing war really is. The book, however, lacks a strong plot. It is essentially episodic in nature, and as a result it is a bit slower reading than many of Burch's books. Another factor that weakens the story is Kate's golden personality. Like Queenie Peavy, Kate is a spunky and outspoken girl, but Kate lacks the flaws that make Queenie such a believable person. Because Kate is so smart, considerate, athletic, popular, and witty, she does not seem quite real.

The Jolly Witch, an amusing short story published in picture book form, is aimed at six-, seven-, and eight-year-olds. The story's main character, Cluny, is a young and pretty witch who is kicked out of the witch colony for being too jolly. A peddler leaves her with a cranky old woman and her somber son. Cluny takes it upon herself to cheer up these two stick-in-the-muds, and she succeeds with the help of her magic broom. Burch includes many funny incidents in the story, and the plot moves swiftly along its predictable course. *The Jolly Witch* is a fantasy, and perhaps this explains why it is uncharacteristically cute. As Burch himself admits, the book does not measure up to his realistic stories.

In *Two That Were Tough,* Burch also does some experimenting, but in this case his attempts succeed. This is a story about the frustrations associated with growing old, but it is told in such a way that even young children can appreciate it. There are two major characters in the book: Mr. Hilton, the owner of a gristmill, and Wild Wings, a feisty old rooster. Both the man and the rooster are nearing the time when they can no longer take care of themselves, but both treasure their independence. Mr. Hilton's daughter finally convinces Mr. Hilton to come live with her in Atlanta. He decides that if he has to move to Atlanta, he is going to take Wild Wings with him. Although he nearly kills himself in the process, he captures the rooster. Holding the rooster in his arms, he reconsiders his plan and finally accepts the reality of his situation. Burch's story is reminiscent of many folk tales about aging. Like these tales, *Two That Were Tough* contains simple language and profound ideas.

In *The Whitman Kick,* Burch again writes about the early 1940s, but this time he creates believable characters and constructs an interesting plot. The book is about Alan Ponder's friendship with a girl named Amanda. They become friends in the sixth grade when, because of physical problems, they both have to stay indoors during recess. They discover that they share an interest in poetry, especially the poems of Walt Whitman. Their love of poetry never dies, but their friendship does during their junior year in high school. Although this book contains no graphic love-making scenes, the issue of sexuality runs throughout the story. As soon as Alan and Amanda become interested in sex, the dynamics of their friendship change. Alan finds it difficult to continue liking Amanda after she begins dating another boy.

Similarly, he finds it difficult to love his mother after she begins having an affair. His disappointment in Amanda and his mother causes him to go through a period of withdrawal during which time he acts self-righteous and experiences self-doubt. The story is told in first person and is completely convincing. Even the characters' love of poetry rings true. *The Whitman Kick* is a moving and memorable book. Like *Two That Were Tough*, it deserves to be ranked among Burch's best.

Moral Issues Confronted

Alethea Helbig

Sometimes humorous, mostly serious, *Wilkin's Ghost* continues the story of the Georgia farm family, the Coleys, begun in *Tyler, Wilkin, and Skee,* with Wilkin, the middle son, telling of events that occurred three years later. Wilkin befriends fifteen-year-old Alex Folsm, cousin of the no-good Floyds down the way, just returned from Atlanta to which he had fled when accused of stealing from Mr. Larson, a local storekeeper. Wilkin arranges for Alex to live as handyboy with the Todd sisters and persuades Mr. Larson to allow Alex to work off the supposed theft. Alex convinces him that living in Atlanta would be great, and Wilkin looks forward to enjoying some of the world's wonders when he learns that this trust has been misplaced, that Alex is not only guilty of the theft from Mr. Larson but has recently stolen twice more, one theft resulting in the death of a neighbor woman.

Wilkin's reasons for helping Alex are never clear, but undoubtedly stem from his perceptions of life and his upbringing. Perhaps Wilkin is moved by a genuine belief in the boy's innocence. Perhaps he helps Alex, at least in part, because of the older boy's charming personality. Perhaps Wilkin just wants to believe in Alex. Perhaps it's the need to make a go of something completely on his own. Perhaps it's simple goodness of heart and the desire to live up to the standards of neighborly conduct he's seen modeled all his life. Wilkin remarks, "It somehow seemed my moral duty. Recently we had talked in Sunday School about people who claim to be so upright and good when they're at church but who don't live up to their religion during the rest of the week"(55).

But pride seems an important motivational factor, too. A bit later, Wilkin humorously notes, "Proud of my noble intentions, I walked away whistling the hymn 'Rescue the Perishing' "(55). Whatever his

Moral Issues Confronted 57

motives for wanting to rescue the perishing Alex, Wilkin reveals himself to be a complex person not inclined to verbalize his motives as much as we wish he would. But once he has embarked on his mission of mercy, it is clear why Wilkin continues with it. "When I say I'll do something I usually do it," he says. "That's because I've got determination." He is honest enough to add, however, that "Tyler and Skee call it stubbornness"(6).

Analogies drawn from nature foreshadow failure in rescuing Alex. Wilkin early has doubts about Alex's intentions and veracity. When Alex begs Wilkin not to tell that he has returned to the area, Wilkin remarks:

> We looked at each other, and there was an expression in his eyes that worried me. It reminded me of a stray dog I once found on the far side of our pasture, caught in barbed wire. While I untangled the wire, the dog, completely shackled, had looked at me as if he were not certain whether I planned to help him or hurt him. When he was free, he had bitten me on the ankle and run off. (46)

Later Miss Etta Todd wonders whether giving Alex a home is a good idea, reminding her sister about a squirrel that they had once nursed to health and that had become everyone's pet. "Then one day Rudie had turned on Miss Julie and bitten her hand"(74).

Wilkin dissembles for Alex, sneaks food to him, worries that Alex may let him down, suspects Alex is making fun of him, yet persists in the relationship. He is not alone in liking Alex, who wins hearts all around, even the irascible, stern storekeeper's. Manipulative, designing, shrewd, Alex turns out to be an excellent student of human nature. He senses that everyone wants to believe him misjudged, and he uses this willingness to forgive and accept to his advantage. At the end, Alex leaves Wilkin to face the music alone. We never learn how Wilkin really feels about the betrayal, but we are confident he will be the better for what has happened. We are certain that both boys will, to paraphrase Cousin Edgar's words, walk in their own integrity (116), Wilkin secure in the love of his family and community and Alex, a maverick never trusted, never loved.

While well-drawn, neither Wilkin nor Alex comes close to beguiling the intellect and emotions as does eccentric and lovable Ida Early, star of two books involving the close and loving Sutton family and also set in rural Georgia, *Ida Early Comes Over the Mountain* and

Christmas with Ida Early. Ida appears inexplicably Mary Poppins-like one morning in mid-July at the Sutton farmhouse, "where nobody had laughed much in recent months"(15). She brings with her her own brand of magic, soon lifting the spirits of the entire Sutton household. A cross between a telephone pole and a scarecrow, unkempt, tall, bony, Ida is unfailingly cheerful and cleverly inventive. She quickly wins the hearts of the four lively motherless children and their soft-spoken, level-headed father, all fed up with Ida's foil, bossy, judgmental Aunt Earnestine, who has been caring for them since their mother died.

Competent and understanding, more than housekeeper, Ida becomes friend, guide, and protector. The children particularly admire her throwing ability, which she first demonstrates to proper Aunt Earnestine's intense disapproval by removing her baggy sweater, twirling it twice about her head, and then whirling it smartly across the room onto the hatrack. "The secret of my good aim's in the wrist movement," she explains proudly (9). Her tall tales about herself enrapture the children. She is tiddlywinks champion of the world, once rode buffaloes on a little red saddle with a white fringe, was the head-knocker cook on a pirate ship—whatever skill the occasion demands Ida claims she's champion of it. The children soon see "that nobody gets the best of Ida"(60). She also has a talent for looking at things as a child does. She knows, for example, that if the Sunday funnies are not read immediately, they're "liable to disappear." She yodels the twins to sleep and allows the children to eat their biscuits by sticking their fingers in them and then filling the hollows with syrup.

Some episodes are funny, some poignant, all are interesting and lively. We get a clear hint of trouble to come when on the way to the fair Ellen remarks that "Ida's an embarrassment sometimes"(63). At school's opening, the twins refuse to attend and Ida has to take them. In the schoolyard, the other children make fun of her. Neither Randall nor Ellen speaks up on her behalf. "Randall knew he should say something, tell their classmates that the joke had gone far enough and to leave Ida alone. But he couldn't speak"(87). Knowing that Ida will probably leave them, Randall and Ellen compose a letter to her: "We will never again fail to come to the aid of someone we love" and put it in her overalls pocket (112). She returns near Thanksgiving, breezing in on a motorcycle, announcing she has missed her "TRUE friends."

The sequel proceeds in much the same vein. Ida has been accepted in the area, despite her eccentricities, or perhaps now because of them. The episodes are unified by the humorous attempts of the twins, and later of others, to promote a romance between Ida and young Preacher Preston, who at story's end may be, but probably isn't, on the way to practicing what he has been taught to preach, instructed by association with Ida Early. Practical Ida notes that he surely seems to like her cooking.

It would be hard to accept Ida's outlandish behavior in the context of a realistic novel were it not for the story's gentle tone and warm humor, the loving, believable depiction of family and community life, and the subtle, telling portrayal of the deep-down hurts and yearnings of one who is different. Ida's stories lack the impact of the novel about Queenie Peavy (there can be only one Queenie, after all), but Ida certainly has her own brand of magnetism. She demonstrates effectively that Robert Burch has a talent for creating memorable characters, particularly in down-home Georgia settings.

The 1987 Phoenix Award Winner

Smith

Leon Garfield

Scrawny, scroungy, eighteenth-century London street urchin Smith picks an old gentleman's pocket of a document, then observes the man killed for the very paper Smith now possesses, whose contents ironically, being illiterate, he cannot read. His efforts to learn to read and to evade the assassins hot on his trail lead him through a convoluted, action-filled, carefully controlled Dickensian plot. It offers a full measure of amazing characters, close encounters, treachery, connivance, and villainy, for grandly entertaining and thematically provocative reading from suspenseful beginning to surprising and thoroughly satisfying conclusion.*

---

*This and the following papers about the 1987 Phoenix Award winner were previously published in *Cross-Culturalism in Children's Literature: Selected Papers from the 1987 International Conference of The Children's Literature Association,* ed. Susan R. Gannon and Ruth Anne Thompson. The Children's Literature Association, 1988.

Acceptance: 1987 Phoenix Award

Leon Garfield

Ladies and gentlemen, first of all I want to thank you for the honor you have done me by awarding the Phoenix to *Smith*, not least because it puts me in the company of Rosemary Sutcliff and Bob Burch. If prizes are to be valued according to the quality of their recipients, then the Phoenix stands very high indeed.

At the moment, I feel at the wrong end of a postcard, inasmuch as my sentiments are not so much, "Wish you were here," as, "Wish I were there!" So I must remain a disembodied voice. But perhaps that is best for a writer. Books, I feel, once written, belong to the reader; and the writer should mind his own business and let the reader's imagination take what it wants. I remember once talking to a school about *Smith*. There was a boy, a fidgeting, restless, disagreeable-looking boy, who, when at last permitted to speak, announced that *Smith* was the book for him. My opinion of him went up and I saw that, far from being disagreeable, he was a most sensitive and intelligent boy, blessed with discrimination and good judgment. Then he went on to tell me why he had liked the book, and, giving way to enthusiasm, he launched upon a splendid exposition of the story, improving on it at several points. Finally, exhausted as much by his own invention as mine, he concluded by saying that it was a very good book and I ought to read it.

I believe it was the same boy—although I like to think it was another for a writer always likes to multiply the number of his admirers—who explained why he thought that *Smith* was a book that had something in it of value for everybody. There was, he said, pickpocketing for boys and sewing for girls.

Smith was a book that cost me a great deal of labor to write. It was my third book; and, as the two previous ones had been first-person narratives, my editor, Grace Hogarth, thought it time I grew up and left the nursery of "I" for the grown-up world of "he." I was thrown into a panic. No longer could I hide my historical ignorance under the convenience of seeing only what one pair of eyes would see. Mistakes made by a first-person are mistakes made by a character, and, to the charitably minded, can seem deliberate. But mistakes made in the third person are mistakes made by the writer himself. So I had to work hard and do a great deal more research, for which I was fitted neither by inclination nor training. Because I never knew where to look precisely for what I wanted, I stumbled upon many an item of queer and out-of-the-way information when looking in quite the wrong place. In fact, many of the episodes in *Smith* arose from just such chance encounters. I only found out about the ventilators in Newgate Prison because I was looking up something else; and although I kept to my original intention to have Smith escape under his sister's skirts, I couldn't resist using the ventilators as well.

I still do research in the same haphazard way. Sometimes people ask me why I don't employ a researcher and save myself time and trouble. The answer is that, apart from the cost, research for a storyteller is like the quest for the right husband or wife. You don't know what you're looking for until you find it.

There now! I think I've talked enough. I'm sure the bar is open, and you all have better things to do. In conclusion, while thanking you again, let me remark on the paradox of awarding a pipe-smoker the Phoenix. Far from rising from the ashes, the ashes most frequently arise from me!

Leon Garfield

Both the career and the writings of Leon Garfield have been wide-ranging. He was born in Brighton, Sussex, in 1921, attended Brighton Grammar School, and studied art before serving in the Royal Army Medical Corps during World War II. From 1946 to 1969 he worked as a biochemical technician at Whittington Hospital, London, and then became a full-time writer for both adults and young people.

His first novel, *Jack Holborn,* uses melodramatic plot, ironic tone, and a wealth of striking metaphors, a pattern of style that distinguishes most of his later published works. His fiction falls roughly into four types: tense period novels set in the eighteenth century with convoluted plots and Dickensian characters; bone-chilling ghost stories combining supernatural events with eerie realism; rollicking farces of mistaken assumptions and misplaced confidence; and picture books, most of them based on folktale or biblical stories. In addition he has written, with Edward Blishen, two unusual retellings of Greek myth and hero tale, both embodying the tension and concrete detail of novels, and a variety of nonfiction, including *The House of Hanover: England in the Eighteenth Century. Child o' War: The True Story of a Boy Sailor in Nelson's Navy* combines biography, history, and fiction in its three-level structure, with quotations from the actual memoirs of a man who joined the British navy as a young child, invented scenes of his dictation in his elderly years of these memoirs to his bored family, and passages giving a broader historical picture of the events in which the child was involved.

Even before the Phoenix Award, Garfield received numerous honors for his writings. In 1981 he was Britain's nominee for the international Hans Christian Andersen Award. *Devil-in-the-Fog* won the Guardian Award for fiction, *The God Beneath the Sea* won the Carnegie Medal, and *John Diamond* won the Whitbread Award. Both *Black Jack* and *The Dummer Boy* were named as commended by the Carnegie committee, and several of his novels were on the *Choice* magazine list of books selected for an academic library and *The Horn Book Magazine* Fanfare list.

For adults Garfield has written *The House of Cards* and a completion of the unfinished novel by Charles Dickens, *The Mystery of Edwin Drood*. He is married to Vivien Alcock, also a writer and artist.

Books by Leon Garfield

Jack Holborn. Illus. Antony Maitland. London: Constable, 1964; New York: Pantheon, 1965.
Devil-in-the-Fog. Illus. Antony Maitland. London: Constable, 1966; New York: Pantheon, 1966.
Smith. Illus. Antony Maitland. London: Constable, 1967; New York: Pantheon, 1967; Penguin, 1968; Dell Yearling, 1987.
Black Jack. Illus. Antony Maitland. London: Longman, 1968; New York: Pantheon, 1969.
Mister Corbett's Ghost. Illus. Alan E. Cober. New York: Pantheon, 1968.
Mr. Corbett's Ghost and Other Stories. Illus. Antony Maitland. London: Longman, 1969.
The Drummer Boy. Illus. Antony Maitland. New York: Pantheon, 1969; London: Longman, 1970.
The Restless Ghost: Three Stories. Illus. Saul Lambert. New York: Pantheon, 1969.
The Boy and the Monkey. Illus. Trevor Ridley. London: 1969; New York: Watts, 1970.
The God Beneath the Sea. With Edward Blishen. Illus. Charles Keeping. London: Longman, 1970; New York: Pantheon, 1971.
The Strange Affair of Adelaide Harris. Illus. Fritz Wegner. London: Longman, 1971; New York: Pantheon, 1971.
The Captain's Watch. Illus. Trevor Ridley. London: Heinemann, 1972.
The Ghost Downstairs. Illus. Antony Maitland. London: Longman, 1972; New York: Pantheon, 1972.
Child o'War: The True Story of a Boy Sailor in Nelson's Navy. With David Proctor. Illus. Antony Maitland. London: Collins, 1972; New York: Holt Rinehart, 1972.
Lucifer Wilkins. Illus. Trevor Ridley. London: Heinemann, 1973.
The Golden Shadow. With Edward Blishen. Illus. Charles Keeping. London: Longman, 1973; New York: Pantheon, 1973.

The Sound of Coaches. Illus. John Lawrence. London: Kestrel, 1974; New York: Viking, 1974.
The Prisoners of September. London: Kestrel, 1975; New York: Viking, 1975.
The Pleasure Garden. Illus. Fritz Wegner. London: Kestrel, 1976; New York: Viking, 1976.
The House of Hanover: England in the Eighteenth Century. London: Deutsch, 1976; New York: Seabury, 1976.
The Apprentices. New York: Viking, 1978; London: Heinemann, 1982.
The Lamplighter's Funeral. Illus. Antony Maitland. London: Heinemann, 1976.
Mirror, Mirror. Illus. Antony Maitland. London: Heinemann, 1976.
Moss and Blister. Illus. Faith Jaques. London: Heinemann, 1976.
The Cloak. Illus. Faith Jaques. London: Heinemann, 1976.
The Valentine. Illus. Faith Jaques. London: Heinemann, 1977.
Labor in Vain. Illus. Faith Jaques. London: Heinemann, 1977.
The Fool. Illus. Faith Jaques. London: Heinemann, 1977.
Rosy Starling. Illus. Faith Jaques. London: Heinemann, 1977.
The Dumb Cake. Illus. Faith Jaques. London: Heinemann, 1977.
Tom Titmarsh's Devil. Illus. Faith Jaques. London: Heinemann, 1977.
The Filthy Beast. Illus. Faith Jaques. London: Heinemann, 1978.
The Enemy. Illus. Faith Jaques. London: Heinemann, 1978.
An Adelaide Ghost. London: Ward Lock, 1977.
The Confidence Man. London: Kestrel, 1978; New York: Viking, 1979.
Bostock and Harris; or, The Night of the Comet. Illus. Martin Cottam. London: Kestrel, 1979; as *The Night of the Comet.* New York: Delacorte, 1979.
John Diamond. Illus. Antony Maitland. London: Kestrel, 1980; as *Footsteps.* New York: Delacorte, 1980.
Fair's Fair. Illus. Margaret Chamberlain. London: Macdonald, 1981; illus. S. D. Schindler. Garden City: Doubleday, 1983.
King Nimrod's Tower. Illus. Michael Bragg. London: Constable, 1982; New York: Lothrop, 1982.
The Writing on the Wall. Illus. Michael Bragg. London: Methuen, 1983; New York: Lothrop, 1983.

The King in the Garden. Illus. Michael Bragg. London: Methuen, 1984; New York: Lothrop, 1985.
Guilt and Gingerbread. Illus. Fritz Wegner. London: Viking Kestrel, 1984.
The Wedding Ghost. Illus. Charles Keeping. Oxford: Oxford, 1985; New York: Oxford, 1987.
Shakespeare Stories. Illus. Michael Foreman. London: Gollancz, 1985; New York: Schocken, 1985.
The December Rose. London: Viking Kestrel, 1986; New York: Viking Kestrel, 1987.
Blewcoat Boy. London: Gollancz, 1988.
The Empty Sleeve. London: Viking Kestrel, 1988; New York: Delacorte, 1988.
Revolution!. London: Collins, 1989.
Saracen Maid. Illus. John Talbot. New York: Simon & Schuster, 1991.

Mystery and Melodrama: Three Novels by Leon Garfield

Agnes Perkins

Smith, Leon Garfield's scruffy, undersized, ignorant hero of his 1967 novel, is a twelve-year-old pickpocket in eighteenth-century London. Smith (he seems to have no other name) is clever and quick—"a rat was a snail beside Smith, and the most his thousand victims ever got of him was the powerful whiff of his passing and a cold draught in their dexterously emptied pockets" (3-4). The chance selection of a country gentleman as his victim leads to a maze of threats and betrayals, for after skillfully lifting the contents of the old fellow's pocket, Smith ducks into a doorway and sees the man murdered and his body searched. After mingling with the crowd and escaping, Smith looks to see that his prize is a document, valuable enough to be murdered for, which he cannot interpret, being illiterate. Because no one of his acquaintance who has skill with letters can also be trusted, Smith sets about trying to find someone to teach him to read.

Before this can be accomplished, Smith is fingered as the holder of the document, and, pursued by the murderers, two sinister men in brown, he runs through London's back alleys and sooty courts, finally eluding them and bumping into a lost blind man, Mr. Mansfield, magistrate, whom the boy in pity leads to his home. Set up in the Mansfield household as assistant groom, with the magistrate's daughter teaching him to read, Smith is accused by an attorney of having killed the old country gentleman, and Mr. Mansfield, whom the boy calls "old Blind Justice," regretfully sends him to Newgate Gaol. From then on their lives are inextricably bound together, with Smith escaping from prison, saving the magistrate in a blinding snowstorm on Finchley Common, and later refusing to abandon him when the real villains discover them in the cemetery at Prickler's Hill.

The story has a breakneck pace, with tense scenes and melodramatic flourishes. Besides following the conventions of the eighteenth-century novel, rich in language and labyrinthine plot, it skillfully enlists the reader's sympathy for an initially unsavory hero. Scenes of the grimy area of London around St. Paul's and Ludgate Hill, as well as the prison itself, are strongly sensory, particularly in smell, and the biting cold of Smith's nights in the streets and on the common is equally vivid. The novel also unsentimentally demonstrates the theme that blind justice must be tempered with compassion.

Smith has been chosen by The Children's Literature Association Phoenix Award Committee as the best book published twenty years ago which did not at that time receive any major award but which has stood the test of the passing years. It is certainly one of Garfield's best novels, showing him as a skillful plotter, a brilliant stylist, and an author capable of inventing a protagonist to whom a reader is drawn emotionally set in a story that considers a theme of depth and complexity.

Two of Garfield's novels that have much in common with *Smith* are *Black Jack*, first published in 1968, and *John Diamond*, published in 1980 and reissued in the United States under the title *Footsteps*. If *Smith* can be viewed as a study of the conflicting demands of justice and compassion, *Black Jack* might be said to be about human bondage, the fears, obligations, and emotions that hold people together against their logical judgment. When Mrs. Gorgandy, a "Tyburn widow" who makes a good thing of claiming bodies of those hanged without any true grieving family and selling them to physicians, needs help handling the huge body of the ruffian Black Jack, she calls upon the pity of a young draper's apprentice, Tolly Dorking, and then tricks him into sitting with the corpse while she rushes off to dicker with prospective buyers. To Tolly's horror, the body begins to move and make some choking noises and—by signs—to get him to pull a silver tube from its throat, which Black Jack has inserted himself to thwart the hangman. From then on Tolly is in the power of the giant, linked to him by mutual fear, Black Jack's that Tolly will turn him in to be hanged properly, and Tolly's that Black Jack will murder him or other innocent victims if he tries to get away.

When Black Jack puts a large stone in a turn in the road where it will certainly cause a coach to upset, planning to get a reward for helping right it or to rob the passengers, the first to overturn spills out an unusual cargo. It is Dr. Jones, who runs a private madhouse in

Islington, and his newest inmate, a mentally disturbed girl named Belle Carter, being sent by her wealthy family to be kept out of sight so that her older sister can marry into a titled family without their secret shame being discovered. Belle escapes to a nearby wood. Tolly goes to find her, and together they wander on, Belle alternating between sweet, childish prattle and fits of violent temper. They join a traveling fair, where Dr. Carmody, who sells the Elixir of Youth, takes them in, convinced that his quack medicine can cure the girl. To Tolly's horror, Black Jack joins the group, planning to take Belle to the madhouse to collect a reward, but Tolly discovers the giant's weak point: he is terrified of madness and dare not take the girl by force. As Belle's mind clears with good treatment, Tolly finds himself a victim of his own contending emotions, dreading the fate of being caretaker of a madwoman yet drawn to Belle with what becomes deep and overpowering love. His feelings toward Black Jack are also contradictory, made up of fear and hate and a longing for admiration rather than scorn from the huge villain. Through the rest of the book these three break away from and are drawn back to each other in a complex plot that includes blackmail, horrifying scenes in the madhouse, and the public panic as an earthquake seems to presage the end of the world prophesied by a street preacher.

John Diamond is equally melodramatic, with stronger elements of mystery. Night after night, twelve-year-old William Jones has been awakened by the sound of footsteps in the room below his, as his dying father paces the floor. Stricken by conscience, he believes his father is "dying of a worthless son." Hearing the footsteps suddenly stop one night, he creeps down, and his father gives him his gold watch and confesses that he is weighted down by a long-concealed sin: he cheated his friend and partner, Alfred Diamond, and fears he may have caused Diamond's death. Next day he is dead, and William's obnoxious uncle accuses the boy of stealing the watch. Frantic with grief and hatred, William runs off to London, determined to find Mr. Diamond, who, he is sure, will somehow vindicate him.

In London, he becomes involved with a number of Dickensian characters and blunders through a series of ludicrous situations, sinister intrigues, and chilling adventures in which no one is quite what he seems. William, whose first-person narration depicts him as far from perfect, is a naive and sympathetic character, and Garfield's style, as always, is highly individual and skillful. The theme that appearances are often far different from reality is one that recurs in many of the author's books, as does the mixture of melodramatic adventures lightened by ironic, often biting, wit.

These three novels exemplify one aspect of Garfields's writing. Even if he had not achieved distinction in other types of books, these alone would be enough to merit a memorable place in children's literature.

Comedy and Social History in Books by Leon Garfield

Mark I. West

In *Smith,* Leon Garfield explores the underside of eighteenth-century England. It is a book about pickpockets, prisoners, and an array of other characters who exist on the fringes of society. In *The Strange Affair of Adelaide Harris,* Garfield returns to eighteenth-century England, but this time his characters are a bit more affluent, if not more respectable. The central characters are two twelve-year-old boys: Harris, a clever but mischievous son of a prominent physician, and Bostock, a not-so-clever son of a retired ship captain. Like Tom Sawyer and Huck Finn, Harris and Bostock have a close but somewhat lopsided friendship. The two are nearly inseparable, but it is usually Harris who takes the lead. One day their teacher happens to mention that the Spartans sometimes exposed their unwanted infants to the elements, and Harris finds this idea intriguing. He decides to try it out with his baby sister, Adelaide. It is not that he wants to dispose of her, he explains to Bostock; he just wants to see if she will be taken in by a kindly wolf or some other wild animal. They leave little Adelaide in a wooded area where she is soon discovered by a young woman and her suitor. Much to the suitor's chagrin, the young woman decides to rescue Adelaide. What follows is a hilarious comedy of errors complete with a duel, a love affair, and a mysterious private investigator who misinterprets every clue he unearths. It is a lively and amusing book about two lively and amusing boys.

Eight years after the publication of *The Strange Affair of Adelaide Harris,* Garfield published a second book about these boys. The English edition bears the title *Bostock and Harris* while the American edition is called *The Night of the Comet.*

In this book, the boys have aged a year and are beginning to take an interest in girls. Bostock has a crush on Harris's sister Mary, but he has no idea how to win her affections. Harris agrees to help his friend for a price. Bostock's father owns an expensive telescope which Harris wants in order better to see a comet that will soon pass over England, and he insists that Bostock give him the telescope as payment for his advice. As it turns out, though, Harris's advice is not worth much. Everything he knows about courtship is from an article about the mating habits of animals, and the boys soon learn that girls are not necessarily attracted to the some things that attract females of other species. Like *The Strange Affair of Adelaide Harris,* the book is filled with ridiculous situations and complicated plot twists, but through it all Harris and Bostock somehow manage to preserve their friendship.

Garfield has clearly mastered the art of telling a comedic tale, but not all of his books belong to this genre, and *The Apprentices* is one that does not. First published in 1976, this book consists of twelve loosely connected stories, all of which deal with the experiences of apprentices living in eighteenth-century London. These young people work for a variety of masters, including a lamplighter, a midwife, and a pawnbroker. Most of these apprentices are not quite as destitute as Smith, but they tend to have more in common with Smith than with Harris and Bostock. Like Smith, they do not have happy and carefree childhoods. For seven years, they must spend most of their time at work. Still, as Garfield makes clear, they are more than the jobs that they perform. They are also emotional beings, and it is upon this aspect of their lives that most of the stories are focused. In *Moss and Blister,* for example, Garfield describes the bitter disappointment that one ambitious apprentice feels upon learning that his master's wife has finally given birth to a baby boy. The apprentice had planned to marry one of the master's daughters and eventually inherit the business, but with a son in the picture his hopes for a secure future instantly evaporate.

In all three of these books, Garfield shows that he is as concerned with the complexities of human nature as he is with the complexities of English social history. This is one of the reasons why his historical fiction so often succeeds in touching the hearts of his readers.

Retellings from Greek Mythology and Picture Book Stories by Leon Garfield

Taimi M. Ranta

Leon Garfield, a prolific author for nearly a quarter-century, has become recognized as a leading British historical novelist for young people, surpassed only by Rosemary Sutcliff. Often his setting has been the eighteenth century, his atmosphere Dickensian, his characters experiencing a rags-to-riches change. However, in the early 1970s Garfield turned to retellings of Greek mythology and in the early and middle 1980s to picture books, these often retellings of Bible stories.

In 1970, he published his Carnegie Award-winning *The God Beneath the Sea* and in 1973 *The Golden Shadow*. Both were co-authored by Edward Blishen, a man well-versed in Greek myths, and an editor and friend.

The God Beneath the Sea is a retelling of Greek myths, framed with the two violent expulsions of Hephaestus from Olympus by each of his cruel and angry parents. The two authors attempt to restructure the collection of myths into a continuous narrative. They divide their work into three sections: "The Making of the Gods," "The Making of Man," and "Gods and Men."

In "Part One: The Making of the Gods," Garfield and Blishen begin with the account of the ugly infant Hephaestus's expulsion from the heavens when his mother, Hera, rejects him. The authors follow the myth found in the *Iliad* which makes Hephaestus the first child of Hera and Zeus and has him cast out of heaven and down into the depths of the sea by his mother because of his monstrous deformities. The goddesses of the sea, Thetis and Eurynome, become his guardians, protecting and raising the deformed child. As they tell him the history of the gods beginning with the birth of the Titans and continuing through the birth of his own brothers and sisters, they reveal the history of Olympus. Part One concludes with Ares's birthday party when Hephaestus is restored to Olympus and is granted the beautiful Aphrodite, "the magical goddess of desire" (72), as his wife, which follows closely the story found in the *Odyssey.*

"Part Two: The Making of Man" recounts Prometheus's creation of man from clay. Prometheus, in defiance, does not follow Zeus's order to destroy his creation, but instead gives man the gift of fire. Zeus, greatly angered, does not strike out against Prometheus immediately, but rather bestows on him the gift of lovely Pandora as a wife. Through her, mankind will suffer opposition of their own passions as they mingle with the gods. Prometheus is then thrown into chains and besieged by the vicious vulture who is to torment him by day.

"Part Three: Gods and Man" relates the mingling of gods with mankind. The bulk of this section includes the retelling of the story of Persephone, the child of Demeter and Zeus, and her fate to live in the underworld with dark Hades, and that of Autolycus, child of Chione and Hermes, and his rivalry with Sisyphus. Garfield and Blishen conclude the work with Zeus's overthrow by Hera and their children. With the help of the sea goddess Thetis and the hundred-handed giant Briareus, Zeus is freed and wreaks revenge on his wife and children. Zeus then flings Hephaestus, who is sympathetic to Hera's plight, out of Olympus again. When readers have finished the book they have been exposed to a sweeping narrative from the Titans to the birth of Odysseus and the building of Troy.

This piece of fiction is written in a poetic style befitting the passionate tales it relates. The ugly and violent passions of the Titans in Part One are equalled by the tender and compassionate emotions felt by Prometheus for his little creatures in Part Two. The authors weave the two worlds of gods and men together briefly in Part Three. Although the beauty of their style is appreciated by some, Garfield and Blishen frequently sacrifice clarity in an effort to link so many myths into a flowing narrative. Often too many characters create confusion, and the text has to be read slowly, with frequent references to Hamilton or Bulfinch for clarification. Its swift pace, the compacting of so much in so short a work, and the authors' seeming assumption that the reader already has substantial knowledge of mythology limit the book's audience.

The Golden Shadow by Garfield and Blishen is a more satisfactory experience for a wider range of readers. This recreation of Greek legends is easier to follow and is quite beautifully written. The unity of the book is provided by "a poet, a storyteller, who collected tales that he wove into ballads for the entertainment of any who'd clothe and feed him" (12). *The Golden Shadow* traces the history of Heracles from birth to death, giving an account of four of his twelve labors (the slaying of the Nemean Lion, the killing of the Hydra, the cleaning of the stables of Augeas, and the abduction of the dog Cerberus from Hades). The prophecy that Thetis would bear a son greater than his father is witnessed by the storyteller and is also woven throughout the story of Heracles. As the storyteller spends his life following the life of Heracles, he himself longs to understand the prophecy he has witnessed and to actually see a god. He eloquently bemoans the fact that "the pursuit of knowledge had blinded him" and he has "lost the power to behold the divine: and worse, almost the strength to believe in it" (16).

Although the storyteller is a literary device to link the myths being retold and gives unity to the work, he also supplies the mode through which the theme of the work is developed. He exemplifies man's constant searching for the gods, who are always slightly out of reach. Only in death does the storyteller finally see Hermes, who comes to carry him away. Hermes reassures the storyteller that his lifelong hero, Heracles, has been restored to life on Olympus and properly rewarded for his many years of struggles.

This work is well-crafted, and the constant presence of Zeus, "the golden shadow," is artfully presented. For good readers at the high school level who are interested in mythology, this could be a rewarding reading experience.

Neither *The God Beneath the Sea* nor *The Golden Shadow* can be thought of as source material, and, as Clara Hulton pointed out in *Library Journal,* they do not take the place of Colum, Benson, Hamilton, and Graves (2137). But, then in the Afterword of the British edition by Longman, the authors point out that they wanted to produce "a piece of fresh fiction out of some of the oldest tales in the world." That they did.

Mixed reactions have been elicited by the two titles. In *Contemporary Literary Criticism,* it is noted that "The modern interpretations of Greek myths which Garfield wrote with Edward Blishen have been especially criticized for their loftiness and for losing the significance of the myths in the psychological theorizing of the authors"(215). In the *New Statesman,* Alan Garner called *The God Beneath the Sea* "very bad." "It is almost impossible to read, let alone assess," he added (606-7). *The Bulletin of the Center of Children's Books* recommended its reading for grades eight and up, and described it generally as "a stunning book" with "a fluent imaginative style" (56).

The God Beneath the Sea won the prestigious Carnegie Award in 1971 and is one of the most controversial of all Carnegie Medal Awards to date. When asked in an interview if it was ironic that he had won the coveted prize for *The God Beneath the Sea* and not for one of his other books, Garfield replied, "Aggravating rather than ironic" (Wintle 204).

All of Garfield's five picture books are oversized and extravagantly illustrated. The first, *Fair's Fair,* is one with his Dickensian touch, set in snowy London right before Christmas. Two orphaned street waifs are both led to an elegant, deserted mansion by a large fierce-looking black dog. There they eat mysteriously appearing meals, together clean and take care of the place, and even share their food with others. On Christmas Eve, two sinister-looking men appear with the seeming intent to burglarize, which the children avert. The happy ending proves them to be the owner and his lawyer who conveniently have been looking for two such kind, brave, honest, and generous children to adopt. *Fair's Fair* is a sentimental book with large, conventional, detailed illustrations in full color by S. D. Schindler to set the mood for a satisfying story, especially around the Christmas season.

Then came three picture books that are retellings of Bible stories: *King Nimrod's Tower, The Writing on the Wall,* and *The King in the Garden.* They are all illustrated in grandiose style by Michael Bragg.

King Nimrod's Tower is based on the story of the Tower of Babel from the King James Version of the Bible. In this unusual variation, the author juxtaposes a small boy who is trying very hard to make friends with an unruly puppy and the Tower rising gradually in the background. God doesn't want to destroy the proud Nimrod's Tower because the lad might be injured, but rather He brings about the familiar confusing of tongues. The boy finally succeeds in persuading the puppy to accompany him home and the Tower is abandoned. The full-color illustrations are striking but not in keeping with the time of the story. "The boy and the workmen resemble figures from Breughel, and God looks similar to William Blake's depiction of him," says the *Horn Book* reviewer (510).

The Writing on the Wall is based on the Belshazzar story of the writing on the wall and Daniel's interpretation of the words. Here, too, as in *King Nimrod's Tower,* the events are seen through the eyes of a small boy. Sam, a kitchen boy, is more interested in an old hungry cat, Mordecai, than in the earth-shaking events occurring around him. Bold illustrations in double-page spreads depict the details of the castle, the gross eating habits of the gluttonous guests at something that resembles a medieval banquet more than an ancient feast. They are frequently and annoyingly interrupted by the text. Neither the boy-cat story nor the Belshazzar story stands up well on its own.

The King in the Garden is an adaptation of the Old Testament story of King Nebuchadnezzar's madness. Little, spunky Abigail finds the absent, humiliated, bedraggled king in her garden, groveling in the dirt, eating her grass and flowers, and frightening her fish. She takes him in hand and helps him regain some self-esteem. Many of the illustrations are luminous, with yellow and clearwater green dominating. The events alternate between the garden and the castle, which would be difficult for young children. As Rebecca Ray writes in *School Library Journal,* "The invented detail of this story adds nothing useful or beautiful to the original in the Book of Daniel. The picture book audience is not ready for this 'art imitates life' approach" (54).

Although at first glance, the Bible retellings look inviting and inspiring, upon closer scrutiny and evaluation they do not offer the bedrock essence of these stories found in good Bible story collections. Sumptuous illustrations, inclusion of distracting little subplots with child characters, additional narrative details with something of a contemporary flavor all tend to make these less than really successful retellings of well-known Bible stories.

Garfield's latest picture book is *The Wedding Ghost,* illustrated by the very versatile Charles Keeping, but is currently unavailable in the United States. It uses some elements from the old Sleeping Beauty story "to embroider the truism that man's love is divided between the 'very type of normal and easy' and, if not sinister, at least the strange and unattainable" (Briggs 350). Jack and plain Jill are to be married but he hasn't invited his old nurse to the wedding. Her present draws him from his comfortable wedding preparations and leads him on a strange journey to seek that second bride, a journey on which he encounters the beautiful princess covered with dust. After complications, he does in the end marry his Jill, but "the reconciliation of two such fundamentally opposed impulses runs the risk of being reductive or inconsistent" (Briggs 350). It seems that to instill an old familiar tale with new meaning is not as easy as one might think.

All in all, Leon Garfield's retellings of Greek mythology and his picture books have not been as well received as the body of his work. When he is in his own element, that of historical fiction, his work has more vigor, direction, drawing power, and sense of audience than when he collaborates or when he attempts to give an established story a contemporary twist.

Works Cited

Briggs, Julia. Rev. of *The Wedding Ghost*. *Times Literary Supplement* (29 Mar. 1985): 350.
Garner, Alan. Rev. of *The God Beneath the Sea*. *New Statesman* (6 Nov. 1970): 606-7.
Hulton, Clara. Rev. of *The God Beneath the Sea* and *The Golden Shadow*. *Library Journal* (15 June 1971): 2137.
"Leon Garfield." *Contemporary Literary Criticism* (12): 215.
Ray, Rebecca. Rev. of *The King in the Garden*. *School Library Journal* (Aug. 1985): 54.
Rev. of *King Nimrod's Tower*. *The Horn Book Magazine* (Oct. 1982): 510.
Rev. of *The God Beneath the Sea*. *Bulletin of the Center of Children's Books*. (12 Dec. 1971): 56.
Wintle, Justin and Emma Fisher. *The Pied Pipers*. London: Paddington, 1974.

Leon Garfield's Ghost Stories

Alethea Helbig

Among Garfield's other books are several eerie and mysterious ghost stories. Two are full-length novels: *Devil-in-the-Fog,* which concerns an unusual family of traveling actors and won the first Guardian Award, and *The Drummer Boy,* which effectively strips away the glamour from war. Two novelette-length books improvise upon the Faustian legend: *Mister Corbett's Ghost* and *The Ghost Downstairs.* All display the Garfield hallmarks of eighteenth-century settings; distinctive, exuberant, sensory style; intricate plots full of carefully controlled, deliberately melodramatic events that lead to unexpected endings; ironic humor; moral complexities; and elemental themes of greed, hatred, vengeance, illusion, and deception.

Like most Garfield books, *Devil-in-the-Fog* defies brief summarization. George, the fourteen-year-old narrator, enjoys life as the eldest son in the Treet family, an irrepressible troupe of strolling players praised with immodest candor by George as some of "the most talented personages in England." One misty November a "dark and devilish" Stranger calls in the "unwholesome bargain eating away at my father's soul" and plunges George into the strange, new role of real-life heir apparent to family-proud Sir John Dexter. Sir John is embroiled in a Cain and Abel feud with his brother, Richard, whom George soon encounters skulking in a copse on the Dexter estate, a tattered, worn, and pathetic fugitive from Newgate, certainly not the villain George expected. Aiding and advising Richard is the curiously ambiguous Mrs. Montagu, sometime necromancer to Lady Dexter. Mrs. Montagu has called up from the grave an infant "she swore was the spirit of George Dexter," now seemingly a "wicked, wicked ghost" that has prevaricated about his identity.

Though the book's center doesn't produce the emotional pull promised by the beginning and the conclusion is overly extended, a full measure of excitement transpires before George and the reader make important discoveries. In addition to learning who his father is, George finds that things in the real world are not always as they seem and that the accoutrements of a gentleman do not in themselves a gentleman make. Vain, posturing, ambitious, a self-professed genius, George, to his credit, tries hard to please the Dexters. Given the challenge, he seeks to ferret out the truth, though the effort endangers his life.

He has mixed feelings about flamboyant, unpredictable Mister Treet, the book's other most interesting figure. Catching George's bitter uncertainty about returning to Mister Treet, when the latter has been acknowledged George's true father, Lady Dexter helps the youth put things in perspective: "Now you've discovered Mister Treet is not the blackest of villains, dear George, don't be mortified that he's not the brightest of saints, either! There's something in between, you know! So forgive him—for I'm sure he's great man in spite of it all!" (203). And George forgives and accepts his father for the good he knows is there, puts the man's shortcomings out of his mind, and rejoices to leave the manor and return to the troupe, his "golden past to be . . . [his] golden future as well," and the eight Treet geniuses are together again.

The Drummer Boy also involves delusion, illusion, and deception. Complex in ideas like *Devil*, stylistically and structurally it is more tightly knit and hence more emotionally engaging. Charlie Samson, army drummer boy, and five red-coats are the sole survivors of ten thousand soldiers "quite harvested by ambush" on a battlefield in France. They make their way through their fallen comrades, he drumming as they "talked and robbed and talked and robbed." Haunted by the specter of a dead soldier, Charlie travels to London to deliver a message to one Miss Sophia Lawrence, who turns out to be the daughter of the defeated general. Hopelessly enamored of her, Charlie perjures himself to save her father, then discovers that this idol also has feet of clay. His salvation comes from unexpected quarters: the opportunistic surgeon, Mister Shaw, who has conceived an ambiguous fondness for Charlie, and Charity, Miss Sophia's sensible, forthright serving wench, whom Charlie has hitherto scorned. The whole culminates in a smashing chase in New Forest and concludes with Charlie splitting his drumskin, which signifies entry into manhood, and then leaving arm-in-arm with Charity.

Irony supports themes well but distances us from the protagonist. Charlie lacks definition; he is less interesting than his flamboyant counterpart, George Treet. Faceless, stupidly innocent, he is a shallow type who perpetuates his own deception. Having gone to war "to find something to be worthy of," he learns the survivors among the soldiers he idolized are alive because they fled and hid in ditches during the fighting, the general to whom he dedicated his drumming is pompous, self-aggrandizing, and unnaturally attached to his beautiful daughter, and the beauty of the daughter to whom Charlie has given his untarnished devotion masks a cruel, haughty, life-destroying ugliness. Yet Charlie remains doggedly romantic throughout. When he changes, he changes expectedly, and his entry into adulthood, though motivated, seems abrupt. His departure from the forest with Charity "on his arm—and charity deep in his heart"—the novel's final words—usher him into another romantic world, a happy-ever-after conclusion to the novel that offers hope but disquiets the thinking reader.

Scenes are memorable, their pictures sharp, their language energetic and rich with imagery. The ironically poetic and visually vivid opening in present tense—"the scarlet men are marching. The hillside is in bloom with them . . . mounting as if to capture the sun,"—establishes the romantic tone, sets in stark relief the horror of the ambush and the earthiness of the body robbing soon to follow, and contributes universality. Mister Shaw, the grotesquely comic surgeon, "gray and fat, with little frightened eyes," wastes no time as he prudently scours the battlefield "gathering teeth, fine, fresh teeth. Teeth for the toothless back home. Teeth for the ladies; teeth for the gentlemen—at upwards of two pound ten a gnasher" (16). Though not without shortcomings, *Drummer* stands out for the skill with which it is composed.

In *Devil* and *Drummer,* the supernatural forces provide atmosphere. In *Mister Corbett's Ghost* and *The Ghost Downstairs,* two finely cut gems that outshine these two predecessors, the ghosts become functioning characters in their own right. *Mister Corbett's Ghost* echoes the tale of Scrooge as it plays twists and turns on the theme of unholy bargain. One New Year's Eve, willful, defiant Benjamin Partridge, apothecary's apprentice and aspiring celebrant, is ordered by his hard-driving master, Mister Corbett, to deliver a mixture to a little, old, black-garbed man about whom there is "an unmistakable smell of graveyards." Obliged to walk three miles through the dark and cold, despairing and raging ("Nails in your coffin, Mister Corbett"), Benjamin repairs to a secluded house on the heath and concludes with the same little old man a bargain for Mister Corbett's death. When the corpse and then the ghost become unmanageable, he opts for an unselfish act that redeems both him and Mister Corbett, and Benjamin welcomes the New Year, relieved to have his master in the flesh again. He has learned that the cost of irresponsible action may come high and that forgiveness is sweeter than revenge.

We feel little sympathy for complaining, surly Benjamin at story's start, and still less when he initiates his dark agreement. But the discipline of suffering he undergoes changes his outlook substantially and draws us to him. We disapprove his attempts to justify himself. "You brought it on yourself, Mister Corbett. You were as hard as iron," he asserts unhappily. We think better of him when remorse sets in and he acts compassionately for the piteous ghost. When he realizes the ghost can "give but terror and freezing cold" and that there is no place for the *two* of them to go "in their misery and their shame," we see how much he has changed and share his suffering.

At the very end, when Benjamin "begins to wonder whether his dark venture had been a dream," we, too, wonder. The third person focus is so tight it gives the effect of "I" narration. Maybe, we think, this has all taken place in Benjamin's head, a figment of the overwrought imagination of a rebellious adolescent. But so vividly does Garfield draw the ghost, so tormented is the specter ("Hell is cold . . . ," he pleads), so clearly realized is the ironic murderer, that we have no difficulty accepting the events as actually happening, the ghost as real as Benjamin. Along with Benjamin we conclude that the evil we do has its origin within us.

The macabre in the allegorical sense hinted at in *Mister Corbett's Ghost* is more fully realized in *The Ghost Downstairs*. Mr. Fishbane, new neighbor below, reeks of sulphur. Since he also reeks of wealth, Mr. Fast, sharp-minded solicitor's clerk, cultivates his friendship. Supremely confident of his ability to outwit the old man legally, he draws up a contract in which in return for a million pounds he will give the old man his soul and seven years of the end of his life, a contract signed not in blood, but with beetroot juice, and hence "red in tooth and clause." Even though the fine print specifies the first seven years of his life, Mr. Fast soon feels uneasy with his bargain. He notices a dark and shadowy shape accompanying his benefactor, which slowly and horribly materializes as a sad-eyed, pallid-faced, little boy dressed in an old-fashioned sailor suit. Mr. Fast has bargained away his own childhood, and with it his hopes and dreams, rendering, ironically, the million pounds of no value. What good is money without dreams for it to satisfy? Dismay and fear progress relentlessly into terror when Mr. Fishbane grants the ghost-child's fondest wish, to drive a train, which to his horror Mr. Fast soon realizes is a death train. He halts it, saving the passengers at the cost of his own life, and is thus redeemed from his unholy bargain.

Mr. Fast is more repulsive at the beginning than is Benjamin Partridge. The grasping solicitor's clerk appears to have no redeeming qualities. We are introduced to him in a sardonically witty passage: "Two devils lived in Mr. Fast—envy and loneliness. Together they gnawed at him, drained the color from his face, the luster from his eyes and the charity from his heart" (3).

A little later we are told that avarice became a "welcome tenant," too, who "got on famously with the two devils . . . all three of them held parties in his head, and dined off Mr. Fishbane's estate" (9). His pride, greed, and arrogance continue to repel us. We dislike him intensely when he attempts to purchase the child's dreams (his own, that is) with the gift of a silver running hoop. The pivotal scene, where we begin to feel sympathy, occurs when he gives his arm to an old woman and helps her through the fog to the train, a Boy Scout act that epitomizes childhood virtue and hints that his discipline of suffering has awakened a decency dormant since childhood. When he is convinced that "the phantom child was fixed on destroying him and . . . was driving the train to destruction," he undertakes to save the glimpse of the phantom at the controls, through Mr. Fast's anguished plea, "Take everything back! Take all my soul—only stop the train!," through the poignant death scene, after which the child speaks as father of the man, whispering, "My son . . . oh, my son . . . ," to conclude with poetic ambiguity. But the end leaves us to ponder the identity of Mr. Fishbane and the phantom child:

> "Come, Dennis," murmured the old man. "Come away, my dear."
>
> Then this weird pair—the shabby old man and the little boy in the sailor suit—drifted away from the glowing scene and seemed to mount the embankment and so dissolve in the upper reaches of the night.

"Where shall we go now?" whispered the little phantom, its pale face smiling up into the old man's.
"God knows," answered Mr. Fishbane, and his beard streamed out to catch the stars. (107)

Perhaps Mr. Fishbane isn't the devil at all. Perhaps the only devil is in Mr. Fast's baser nature. Perhaps, as in *Mister Corbett's Ghost,* the evil people do only originates with them.

This brief discussion has merely sampled the surface texture of these four rich and deeply satisfying books. There is no time here to discuss such aspects as tone, color, the orchestration of rhythm and pace, the wit, the wordplay, the imagery and their effect on characterization, plotting, and atmosphere. Garfield is a master craftsman, whose work, I believe, has not received the attention it deserves on this side of the Atlantic. His books are not simply good reading entertainment. They give us perceptive insights into human nature and the way things are in the world, and at the same time they enhance our appreciation for the delight that beautiful writing brings.

The 1988 Phoenix Award Winner

The Rider and His Horse

Erik Christian Haugaard

Shrewd and observant David ben Joseph, 14, the son of a rich Jewish wine merchant of Tyre, becomes involved in the aftermath of the Roman sack of Jerusalem and in events surrounding the Roman siege and capture of the Hebrew-held fortress, the Masada, in 73 A.D. Vivid scene follows vivid scene as David grows in understanding of self and the world around him and clarifies his values. Understatement and economy of words intensify the drama of this account of a dark period in world history and underscore the book's themes of the futility of war and heroics and of the triumph of the human spirit.*

---

*This and the following article, Mr. Haugaard's acceptance, were previously published in *The Child and the Family: Selected Papers from the 1988 International Conference of The Children's Literature Association*, ed. Susan R. Gannon and Ruth Anne Thompson. The Children's Literature Association, 1988.

Acceptance: 1988 Phoenix Award

Erik Christian Haugaard

Stendhal once declared that all his books were tickets in a lottery whose prize was that they would be read a hundred years after his death. Was it only a vain wish for immortality which made him say that? I do not think so, for though immortality might please your descendant, it has little value to you once you rest under your tombstone. No, the fact that the books are read a hundred years after their author is dead means that they have contained some kind of truth. If people in another age, whose customs and conventions are different from those adhered to when you lived, read and enjoy your books, then surely it must be because they contain at least some elements of truth. When my grandfather died, I inherited his English library. It contained all of Mark Twain and Bret Harte, but there were other authors as well, whose names I did not recognize. One of these books had been published in sixteen editions! The author had certainly been popular, and his book highly thought of, but in the lottery of time it had drawn a blank.

I was very pleased when I was told that my book had been thought worthy of receiving the Phoenix Award. Twenty years is one-fifth of the century Stendhal demanded, and it will have to do. Happily it is not after my death, but twenty years after the birth of the book so I am still around to say thank you.

I admit that there are moments when I watch a movie based upon a book by Thomas Hardy, or see a row of Joseph Conrad's novels in a book store, that I feel a little sad. Both authors while they lived had a hard time finding the money for their daily needs. Conrad copied the whole of *Almyer's Folly* out in longhand, because the original manuscript had been lost. He needed money desperately, and someone had offered to buy it. But you may be sure of one thing: If these authors had been faced with the choice of having their books widely read and bought in their lifetime but never after, or small sales and editions while they lived, but eternal popularity afterwards, they would not have hesitated in making their choice. Still I would have liked to pay a little of my debt, especially to Joseph Conrad, but that is not possible. However grateful we are, we cannot pay their grocery bills in retrospect.

By the time an intelligent person has lived a lifetime, he is—or should be—in debt beyond all calculation. Only the simpleton stays solvent, finding no need to borrow thoughts and ideas from others. He comes into the world poor and leaves it no richer. I think an acknowledgement of that debt is called culture. As the twentieth century draws near to its end, I am a little afraid of the future. Too many young people seem attracted to the solvency of ignorance rather than the debt of culture. Disneyland may be worth a visit, but is it a desirable place to have as a permanent address?

Two books of mine are my own favorites, *The Untold Tale* and *The Rider and His Horse*. I was therefore ever so pleased when I found that others shared my taste. *The Rider and His Horse* was also very well received in England. I was amused that my publishers for that book had cut my second name, Christian. My favorite English critique, which appeared in a small Jewish magazine, ended its praise with the words, "the perfect bar mitzvah present." I think that the highest praise possible for a book written by a Gentile.

I walked from Jerusalem to the Masada, though at the time I could not walk as direct a route as my hero must have taken. Like David I came to Ein-Gedi in the early morning, just as the sun had risen. Surely it is one of the most magic places in the world, the narrow valley so green, the air filled with birdsong, and surrounding it the silent desert. I bathed in the pool by the waterfall, just as my hero had done, and then climbed to the top of the valley and there met a fantastic mountaingoat. We stared into each other's eyes for a few seconds, and then it was gone. The Masada itself is awesome, a piece of history left untouched. At least it was when I was there. I understand it is not quite so anymore. If you should ever visit it, please climb it by the snake path. The exertion itself is part of the experience of having been to the Masada.

Hans Christian Andersen once said: "Praise, I live on it!" It is true, praise inspires us and makes us want to work. Writing is such a lonely craft, and because of that one is easily discouraged. I am pleased to be here in Charleston, pleased that you have found one of my books worthy of the honor of being awarded a prize. I thank the committee which made the decision and all the members of The Children's Literature Association here this evening. You have made me very happy. Again, thank you.

Erik Christian Haugaard

In both his life and his writings, Erik Haugaard is a citizen of the world. He was born in Copenhagen, Denmark, in 1923, emigrated to the United States after his parents moved here, served in the Royal Canadian Air Force during World War II, and has lived in Japan and Ireland. He was educated at Black Mountain College, North Carolina, and later studied at the New School for Social Research in New York. The settings in his many historical novels range widely in both time and place. He has also set picture books in the never-never land of marchen and translated the fairy tales of Hans Christian Andersen.

His earliest novels, *Hakon of Rogen's Saga* and its sequel, *A Slave's Tale*, published more than twenty-five years ago, are stories of the late Viking period still widely read today. *Orphans of the Wind* is a sea story involving an attempt to smuggle munitions to the Confederate army in the American Civil War. *The Little Fishes*, considered by many critics to be the best book for children about World War II, is set in Italy, a story of the struggle to survive of children made street beggars by the fighting. A later novel, *Chase Me, Catch Nobody!*, also concerns the conflict against the Nazis, this one following the adventures of a Danish boy in Germany just prior to the outbreak of the war and his rescue of a little Jewish girl who has been living in hiding. Other novels are set in first-century Palestine, sixteenth-century Japan, seventeenth-century England, and eighteenth-century Ireland.

All are thoroughly researched, excitingly plotted, and written in masterful English. All, moreover, are thoughtful in their consideration of important problems, not relying on easy answers or partisan enthusiasm for their themes. They typically are told in the voice of a first-person narrator and usually concern children who lack the ordinary protection of a family, thrown by chance circumstances or historical events into a largely unfeeling and often threatening world.

Many of these books appear on *The Horn Book Magazine* Fanfare list and the American Library Association list of Notable Books for Children. *The Little Fishes* was awarded the Jane Addams Peace

Association Children's Book Award and the *Boston Globe-Horn Book Award*, both highly prestigious honors in literature for children. Haugaard has also been the recipient of the Danish Cultural Minister's Award, the Chapelbrook Foundation Award, and a Japan Foundation fellowship.

Books by Erik Christian Haugaard

Hakon of Rogen's Saga. Illus. Leo and Diane Dillon. Boston: Houghton Mifflin, 1963; as *Hakon's Saga.* London: Faber, 1964.
A Slave's Tale. Illus. Leo and Diane Dillon. Boston: Houghton Mifflin, 1965; London: Gollancz, 1966.
Orphans of the Wind. Illus. Milton Johnson. Boston: Houghton Mifflin, 1966; London: Gollancz, 1967.
The Little Fishes. Illus. Milton Johnson. Boston: Houghton Mifflin, 1967; London: Gollancz, 1968.
The Rider and His Horse. Illus. Leo and Diane Dillon. Boston: Houghton Mifflin, 1968; London: Gollancz, 1969.
The Untold Tale. Illus. Leo and Diane Dillon. Boston: Houghton Mifflin, 1971.
A Messenger for Parliament. Boston: Houghton Mifflin, 1976.
Cromwell's Boy. Boston: Houghton Mifflin, 1978.
Chase Me, Catch Nobody! Boston: Houghton Mifflin, 1980; London: Granada, 1982.
Leif the Unlucky. Boston: Houghton Mifflin, 1982.
A Boy's Will. Illus. Troy Howell. Boston: Houghton Mifflin, 1983.
The Samurai's Tale. Boston: Houghton Mifflin, 1984.
Prince Boghole. Illus. Julie Downing. New York: Macmillan, 1987.
Princess Horrid. Illus. Diane Dawson Hearn. New York: Macmillan, 1990.
The Boy and the Samurai. Boston: Houghton, 1991.
Translator: *The Complete Fairy Tales and Stories of Hans Andersen.* New York: Doubleday, and London: Gollancz, 1974.
Hans Christian Andersen: His Classic Fairy Tales. Illus. Michael Foreman. London: Gollancz, 1976; New York: Doubleday, 1978.

Diversity and Consistency in Erik Haugaard's Novels

Agnes Perkins

Diversity and consistency—two seemingly contradictory qualities—mark the novels of Erik Christian Haugaard. They are diverse in setting, both in time and place, ranging from the first century in Palestine to Italy during World War II, and including, among others, Norway and France in the late Viking period, sixteenth-century Japan, the English Civil War of the sixteen hundreds, the American Civil War of the eighteen sixties, and Nazi Germany in the nineteen thirties. They are consistent in being skillfully written and in embodying variations of the same themes: the vulnerability of children on their own, the importance of compassion in a cruel world, the falsity of heroics and of showy religion, the value of each individual, however lowly in status.

Now The Children's Literature Association has added to Haugaard's list of honors by choosing *The Rider and His Horse* to be the fourth winner of the Phoenix Award, given for a book that won no major recognition at the time of its publication twenty years earlier but that, in retrospect, is deemed to be of high literary quality worthy of recognition.

The Rider and His Horse is not a book destined to easy popularity. It is about a dark and violent period which ends in the fall of the great Jewish-held fortress, the Masada, to overwhelming Roman forces, and it avoids a facile identification of the good and the right with either the defenders or the critics of that defense. The narrator, David ben Joseph, the fourteen-year-old son of a rich wine merchant from Tyre, is in a caravan attacked by bandits, held for ransom, and, when the bandits are mowed down by Roman cavalry, left for dead. He makes his way with some other waifs to Jerusalem which has been sacked by Roman forces, is able eventually to turn his younger companions over to Simon ben Judas, a Levite who is feeding homeless children, and then, being well educated, joins Simon as an assistant and scribe.

A woman named Rachel, older than David, whose children and husband have been killed by the Romans, comes to ask Simon's help in getting her brother's children from the Masada, only to be told that the commander, Eleazar ben Ya'ir, her cousin, will allow no one to leave. After she sets out to the fortress, determined to care for the children there if she cannot get them out, David follows her, becomes a scribe to Eleazar, and witnesses the last days of the defense, when the Romans construct a great ramp, built largely with Jewish slave labor, to bring up their battering rams and destroy the otherwise invincible mountain fort. He reports the terror of the prospect of the defenders falling into Roman slavery and the horror of the order Eleazar gives, that each man shall kill his wife and children, then himself, to rob the Romans of their prize.

Although David escapes, he is left with no certainties. In fact, David and the reader must cope with a number of ambiguities: the conflict between learning and action, the nature of David's love of Rachel, the zealotry of Eleazar, both admirable and destructive. A tone of irony predominates, yet there clearly emerges a theme that war is futile and heroics are full of self-deception.

The Rider and His Horse is a rich and demanding book. There are vivid scenes of the hungry and homeless turned almost animal in Jerusalem, of rioters trying to break down Simon's gate, and of the fanatically religious Essene colony at a desert oasis. Characters are complex and interesting, if not wholly sympathetic. It is a memorable book, and, where it does not produce warm enjoyment, it is almost certain to demand deep respect.

More than fifteen years after *The Rider and His Horse*, Haugaard published *The Samurai's Tale*, a story set in a far different period and part of the world but with interesting parallels. Again there is a child without family in a war-torn country, again a successful siege of a seemingly impregnable fortress, again a hero involved in a campaign that ultimately ends in defeat. This, however, is a world dominated not by an overriding religious zeal but by the ambitions of rival samaurai clans and by elaborate patterns of etiquette and rigid hierarchies of status, even among the lowest servants of the great houses.

The narrator—the protagonist is typically the first-person narrator in Haugaard novels—starts his story when he is four years old, on the day his father, a samurai, is killed and his home is raided by the soldiers of the mighty lord, Takeda Shingen, who also murder his mother, two older brothers, and most of the servants. Because the child amuses Lord Takeda by standing up to the armed soldiers with his little bamboo sword, he is not killed but given to one of the officers. This samurai, Lord Akiyama, a decent and learned man, renames the boy Taro and assigns him to be the lowest of the helpers in the kitchen which cooks for his servants, a post where he must work hard, even as a young child, but where he is treated kindly and always has enough to eat.

The novel traces the gradual rise of Taro to be horseboy, messenger, and eventually samurai in his own right, all shown against the battles and intrigues of the warlords who contend for domination of the area in their struggle to rule all Japan. The action ends with the defeat of the Takeda clan and the narrator, dressed in the rags of a charcoal burner, observing the body of Lord Akiyama, to whom he has become devoted, stripped and crucified upside down in the manner of a criminal. It is not, however, a hopeless ending. The girl whom Taro loves has been saved by his humble servant, and, since the story is told by Taro in his old age, the reader has assurance of his survival.

These two books, *The Rider and His Horse* and *The Samurai's Tale*, exhibit qualities to be found in all of Haugaard's historical fiction: careful attention to detail, strong action without sensationalism, ironic understatement, and a protagonist worth reading about. They are books which should be republished and, we would hope, be more widely read because of the influence of the Phoenix Award.

Haugaard's Norse Tales

Mark I. West

Although born in Denmark, Erik Christian Haugaard soon took an interest in the land that lies to the north of his native country—the land of Leif Ericson, Eric the Red, and the other Vikings who dominated much of Europe during the eighth, ninth, and tenth centuries; the land of Odin, Thor, Loki and the other Norse gods who so troubled many early Christians; the land of Norway. While still a young man, Haugaard learned Norwegian, studied Norse mythology, and steeped himself in the history of the Vikings. This background proved helpful when he began writing novels in the early 1960s. His first novel, *The Last Heathen,* focused on the conflict between Christianity and the Norse religion. He wrote the book for adults, but when he submitted it to Houghton Mifflin, an editor wrote back suggesting that he rewrite it as a children's book. Haugaard reluctantly agreed and so began his career as a children's author.

Hakon of Rogen's Saga, Haugaard's first children's book, came out in 1963. In the book's preface, Haugaard writes, "I have attempted to tell the story of a boy who lived at the end of the Viking period. It was not written for 'youth' in the sense that I have blunted my pen before I started." In saying this, Haugaard means that the ideas in this book are just as complex as the ideas in his unpublished adult novel. The book's plot revolves around a boy named Hakon who lives on a small island off the coast of northern Norway. When Hakon's father, the ruler of the island, is killed in battle, Hakon's uncle seizes power. The uncle proves to be a tyrant, but the islanders lack the courage to overthrow him. At the crux of the story is an examination of the relationship between cowardliness and tyranny. Both the uncle and most of the people over whom he rules are cowards at heart. It is not until Hakon defies his uncle's authority that the islanders realize that they, too, need not be ruled by fear.

Haugaard's second children's book, *A Slave's Tale*, is a sequel to *Hakon of Rogen's Saga*. This time the story is told from the perspective of a former slave girl named Helga. Although Helga had been freed by Hakon, who is now the island's ruler, she finds that the psychological burdens of slavery do not suddenly evaporate at the moment of emancipation. In addition to dealing with slavery, this story also tackles the issue of religious conflict. This aspect of the story comes into play when Hakon, Helga, and some of the other people from the island travel south to France. There they come into contact with Christians who disapprove of their Norse religion, and a violent conflict ensues. In describing this conflict, Haugaard shows that both sides use religion to justify their own brutality.

Hakon, however, learns from this experience. Toward the end of the book he speaks these words of wisdom: "I think it would be far better if man took the bloody sword and called it his own; and to the gods gave the honor of those deeds done from love and the pitying heart" (214).

After the publication of *A Slave's Tale*, Haugaard went for many years before he wrote another book on the subject. In 1982, however, came *Leif the Unlucky*, set in Greenland during the early 1400s. At this time, the Norsemen who had been living in Greenland for half a millennium are on the verge of extinction. The climate is getting colder, their supplies of food and wood are almost exhausted, and the ships from Norway have stopped coming. Against this backdrop, Haugaard writes about the struggle to maintain hope and human dignity in the face of impending doom. The adults in the story have surrendered to despair, leaving the young people to fend for themselves. Without adult leadership, the youngsters look to their own for guidance. Two boys attempt to fill this leadership vacuum. Leif, the central character in the story, offers compassion and reason while Egil, the story's villain, offers brutality and superstition. In some ways, the book is reminiscent of William Golding's *Lord of the Flies*, but there is an element of optimism that runs through *Leif the Unlucky*. Haugaard does not offer much hope for his characters' long-term survival, but at least some of his characters continue to struggle not only against the elements but also against their own inclinations toward savagery.

The Condemnation of War in Three of Haugaard's Books for Young People

Taimi M. Ranta

Research has revealed that the early adolescent period, roughly ages eleven to thirteen, is probably the optimum time to study such social concepts as war and peace. Erik Christian Haugaard's books stand out for their superior literary merit and their potential for helping young people understand that no one escapes unscathed when war devastates a land. As a disciplined author of historical fiction, he writes about the futility of war in *The Little Fishes, The Untold Tale,* and *Chase Me, Catch Nobody!*

In *The Little Fishes,* a gripping, dramatic tale, Haugaard, master storyteller, has Guido, a twelve-year-old beggar of Naples, struggle to survive the German occupation of Italy during World War II. Haugaard notes in the Root-Greenlaw interview that the resourceful Guido was inspired by a beggar, a totally self-sufficient individual, whom he and his wife met in Italy in the late 1950s. Also, almost all the incidents in the book were based on stories that they heard about various events in the area during World War II (554). Burke Wilkinson writes in his review of *The Little Fishes* in the *New York Times Book Review* that "Here is war in one of its most tragic aspects—the backwash of battle, and the terror and the trauma it inflicts on the young" (16).

At the beginning of the story in the ironic coin-scrambling scene of the pathetic beggar children, the German officer laughs and Italian captain smiles. The former, characterizing the beggar children of Naples, utters with contempt: "In the unclean waters live the little fishes. Some are eaten; most I believe. But some will escape" (4).

Guido, the narrator of this wartime commentary, is one who manages to escape.

His dying mother's legacy, one of an inner motto, helps him to keep his spirit above the dirt and filth, the hopelessness and degradation of the beggar's life. She had said, "Guido, you must be strong. You are all alone. Be strong as iron . . . But be kind, too: or you will wear yourself and others out. Don't be so strong that you will be lonesome" (48-49).

Guido befriends and takes on the responsibility of two other orphaned beggars, sturdy eleven-year-old Anna and her scrawny four-year-old brother, Mario, when their aunt dies in a bombing raid. With them Guido shares his cave in the steep part of Naples, where his most prized possession is a torn woolen mattress rescued from a bombed-out house. Evicted from this cave which had given Guido some semblance of a home, the three decide to flee the war-torn city and head north to Caserta, Capua, Cassino, and the eventual hoped-for shelter of an already overflowing monastery. The second half of *The Little Fishes* is their odyssey of the 1940s, one season of happiness and several of hunger and suffering at the hands of those who would do them harm. Mario dies but Guido and Anna survive, and as Guido says, when they face the uncertain future: "We shall always stay together" (214).

In her review in *Growing Point,* Margery Fisher states that "Erik Haugaard wants to shock and startle the young with the brutality, the wastefulness of war; but if he is so uncompromising, he is certainly not cynical. He does not show us children corrupted by a homeless life; rather, their essential innocence provides the keynote of a sincere and brave story" (1090). A reader twenty years later would certainly tend to agree with her assessment of *The Little Fishes.*

Wilkinson, as well as others, notes that Guido's insights are sometimes more the mature author's than the young narrator's. An example of these timeless gems is "Everything leaves a little scar: both the good and the bad; and when you grow up then the scars are the story of your life" (16). The insights do not detract from the power of Guido's own story but rather provide another dimension for the more mature reader of the book which can be read and appreciated on different levels of comprehension.

Commenting on the book in his response upon receiving the first *Boston Globe-Horn Book* Award for Excellence in Text, the author points out that "In *The Little Fishes* I wanted to tell not only what happened to the victims of war but also how a person could survive, how in degradation he could refuse to be degraded. Our history books tell about the victories and defeats of armies; I wanted to tell about the defeat and victory of a human being" (14).

Told with compassion, *The Little Fishes,* the story of a courageous, independent Italian boy in the tumultuous 1940s, can stimulate ideas of war and peace that have universal importance in the world of the 1980s in the minds of the current readers. This powerful, moving story presents them with still another dimension of war-wrought suffering, that of a group not in the mainstream of the World War II era literature for young people, which concentrates largely on the Holocaust.

The Untold Tale, an unusual, saga-like account of seventeenth-century Denmark, is told in retrospect by the Old Steward to Christian IV, King of Denmark and Norway. It is the grim story of an impoverished, seven-year-old Danish peasant orphan boy, Dag, when Denmark is at war with Sweden. Dag is the son of small, famine-stricken tenant farmers, struggling for existence on a patch of the King's land. The father freezes to death on his way to the capital for help, and his ill mother dies at home. In the stable, their animals lie dead from starvation. From this desolate situation, the child sets forth to find the King who he trusts will put everything right. The readers accompany Dag across the barren, threatening land to his own death.

Along the way, Dag is befriended by the rough but kind Black Lars, a poacher. When endangered by possible capture, Black Lars sends the child to his wife's cousin, Bodil, a tavern keeper of questionable reputation. On the way Dag meets the narrator, then an ambitious young wandering minstrel, and the two join forces. With Bodil and Bodil's six-year-old daughter, Kirsten, they set out for Christianopolis where Bodil hopes to sell beer and supplies to the troops. Hunger and danger plague them. Peter cannot accept the responsibility he feels for Dag and runs away when the Swedes, led by the youthful Crown Prince Gustavus Adolphus, invade. His conscience makes him return but not in time to save innocent Dag from needless death at the hands of a berserk young soldier who feels he needs blood on his virgin sword.

Paul Heins writes that "the events are presented with powerful immediacy; the characters are vigorously delineated in their suffering, weakness, or evil" (292). Black and white drawings, suggestive of woodcuts, are stark, striking, dramatic, and correlate with the overall power of the text. Thirty-seven years later, Peter, now the King's

The Condemnation of War

Steward, tells the story of Dag, because in the tragic chronicle of the child's short life, lies also "the untold tale" of his own, which is the very core of his development as a human being.

In his epilogue, the narrator does not spell out a moral, as the reader might well expect. Rather he writes: "for the untold tale is an immoral story, a shameful tale of how I committed treason to my own heart. Oh you captains and commanders of men, dismount from your proud horses and walk the battlefields; do not count the dead but look at them; and then, if you dare, claim your victories" (210-211). Such is Haugaard's condemnation of war! A moving experience for the enduring, committed reader, *The Untold Tale* is definitely not a book for the average or reluctant reader.

In *Chase Me, Catch Nobody!*, on his Easter holiday in the spring of 1937, fourteen-year-old Erik Hansen, a Danish schoolboy, reluctantly goes on a school-sponsored trip to northern Germany. None of his friends is going, and he dislikes the teacher in charge. The only son of well-to-do parents, Erik is little interested in the stirring political scene brewing next door. In retrospect, he tells of the experiences that pit him, a politically naive teenager, unwittingly against the machinery of Hitler's Third Reich.

On the ferry to Germany, a frantic, faceless man in a grey raincoat hands him a batch of forged passports, telling Erik where to deliver the package if he does not retrieve it. When Erik sees the man arrested by the Nazi SS, he decides to make the delivery when he gets to Hamburg. Becoming involved in the anti-Nazi underground, he himself becomes the target of an exciting, desperate police chase. In the process of eluding the Gestapo, Erik becomes the guardian of "Nobody," a half-Jewish German girl who has been hiding in a attic for a year. With the help of clever Nikolai, his one new friend on the trip, the three barely manage to escape the pursuing evil Freiherr von Klein in a leaky, broken-down rowboat to the still-free Danish shores—wet, dirty, but safe.

Zena Sutherland acknowledges that *Chase Me, Catch Nobody!* is a good adventure thriller but feels that it is much more than that. She writes that it is "an indictment of a cruel regime" and "a perceptive, smooth development of a growing political awareness of Erik's part, an awareness that stirs a sense of justice, an anger in injustice, a willingness to become involved, and that results in an impressive (and credible) display of courage and initiative" (191).

Concise style, tense pace, vivid, colorful characterization, and schoolboy humor and pranks to relieve the tension make this a very readable book. Jack Forman does complain that Haugaard "interjects many of his opinions and autobiographical adult preceptions into Erik's narrative" and that "some of the many German phrases used can be understood only by context" (124). Actually the so-called opinions and perceptions add strength to the narrative and the use of German, authenticity. *Chase Me, Catch Nobody!* is a skillfully crafted combination of serious theme and fast-action, suspenseful adventure. Set on the very brink of World War II, it gives the reader a perceptive prelude to the many books about this historical period that are available for young people.

Ruth Hill Viguers aptly summarizes Erik Christian Haugaard's contribution to literature for young people: "Mr. Haugaard sets a high standard for books for today's young people. Always he has a story to tell, a powerful story that touches emotions and shows respect for his readers. And, deeply and completely integrated in his story, he has something to say that transcends didacticism, that leaves a residue of wisdom and compassion in the hearts of his readers" (496). This certainly is true of *The Little Fishes, The Untold Tale,* and *Chase Me, Catch Nobody!*

Works Cited

Fisher, Margery. Rev. of *The Little Fishes,* by Erik Christian Haugaard. *Growing Point* 6 (1968): 1090.
Forman, Jack. Rev. of *Chase Me, Catch Nobody!* by Erik Christian Haugaard. *School Library Journal* 26, No. 8 (1980): 124.
Haugaard, Erik Christian. "Thank You Note and Credo." *The Horn Book Magazine* 44 (1968): 14.
Heins, Paul. Rev. of *The Untold Tale,* by Erik Christian Haugaard. *The Horn Book Magazine* 47 (1971): 292.
Root, Shelton L., Jr., and M. Jean Greenlaw. "Profile: An Interview with Erik Christian Haugaard." *Language Arts* 56 (1979): 549-61.
Sutherland, Zena. Rev. of *Chase Me, Catch Nobody!* by Erik Christian Haugaard. *Bulletin of the Center for Children's Books* 33 (1980): 191.
Viguers, Ruth Hill. "Quest, Survival, and the Romance of History." *A Critical History of Children's Literature.*

Ed. by Cornelia Meigs. Rev. ed. New York: Macmillan, 1969.

Wilkinson, Burke. Rev. of *The Little Fishes,* by Erik Christian Haugaard. *The New York Times Book Review, Part II* (7 May 1967): 14, 16.

On Three Works by Erik Haugaard: *Prince Boghole, A Boy's Will,* and *Orphans of the Wind*

E. Wendy Saul

A boy, seemingly alone in the world. Eric Haugaard plays with this image in three books addressed to young people of varying ages, set in different times and places.

The newest of these, the picture book *Prince Boghole,* is a slightly irreverent look at three fairy tale suitors, each vying for the hand of the lovely Princess Orla. Her father, King Desmond, "had reached an age when even a golden crown rests heavily on the head." He contacts his counterparts in Leinster and Ulster to see if they have a son capable of managing a kingdom and winning the love of his daughter. During the interim a third young man, Prince Brian, arrives at the castle gate. His raven hair pleases the princess and his speech pleases her father. But the servants "titter softly" at the youth's shabby clothes and one of them whispers, "His father's kingdom is a bog, only good for cutting turf. Let's call him Prince Boghole."

Needless to say, Princess Orla likes neither of the other rich princes nearly as well as the altogether bright, energetic and pleasant Brian. In a test of wisdom all three are sent to "bring back the bird he thinks is most wonderful." A year and a day later the overbearing Prince of Ulster returns with an eagle, the foppish Prince of Leinster with a peacock, and belatedly in strolls the ragged Brian with a "drab, colorless" nightingale. The wise nursemaid Gormlai asks each to have his bird sing, and Brian, somewhat the worse for wear, wins the contest and is wed to the overjoyed Orla.

Although this is surely a story dipped from the well of happily-ever-after, it is interesting to note Brian is not a wealthy prince in disguise, but rather a boy who without money or connections (even the servants sneer at him) finds a creative solution to an archetypal riddle and achieves what others with material resources are unable to garner. Brian's victory is not just the result of his own ambition, for each of the suitors searches far and wide. Instead, he wins because the wise nursemaid develops a test she knows he can pass and, furthermore, defines success in terms which highlight only his achievement. The book is playful, reassuring, but also makes an telling statement about the importance of finding moral, sensible, and kind allies outside of the family.

A Boy's Will, a work of historical fiction appropriate for elementary school age children, takes place during the American Revolution on and around the Irish island of Valentia. The protagonist, a handsome, thirteen-year-old orphan, Patrick, lives with his paternal grandfather. The boy's mother had not managed to leave him much besides his good looks and popish heritage, and his father was lost at sea some three years before the story opens. The grandfather, a smuggler and drunkard, talks disparagingly of Patrick's Catholic mother, and gives the boy little respect.

Patrick has long overheard discussions of the American colonies' dissatisfaction with the taxation laws, and sides with those, like the Irish, who are held in contempt by the imperialistic British. His sympathy for the rebels finds an outlet when the youngster learns that a decoy ship has been set up in his own harbor to ambush a small American fleet. Patrick decides to warn John Paul Jones, captain of the American flotilla. The boy is aware that this action has consequences: warning the Americans is tantamount to cutting off all ties to his past. After a harrowing chase at sea, the lad escapes his grandfather, is taken on board the American frigate, and is rewarded with the praise of John Paul Jones himself.

Patrick, like Prince Boghole, is a boy without wealth or family who manages to make his way in the world. And even in this seemingly realistic work, the appeal of familial ties is neatly obviated by the peculiar circumstances of Patrick's life—there is a conspicuous absence of caring and love at "home." In fact, one could argue that Patrick took up the American cause in defiance of his grandfather. Still, the boy might well have "come of age" simply by leaving to seek his fortune; instead Haugaard uses moral outrage as the force which finally propels Patrick to action. The adolescent searches not for wealth or love, the stuff of which fairy tales are made, but for a new community where his ideas and bravery will be valued.

The highly acclaimed *Orphans of the Wind* is the most complex of the three works cited here. The tale begins in Bristol, England, where twelve-year-old Jim, again an orphan, has been left in the custody of his miserly uncle and aunt, characters who share much in common with the most scurrilous Dickensesque villains. The uncle lies about the boy's age to the captain of a ship loaded with cargo for America who signs the child up as cabinboy. In this conspicuously male world Jim learns to differentiate among the adults in his midst— to trust the kind and wise cook, Rolf; to despise the unscrupulous captain; and to fear the insanity of a scripture-quoting deckhand.

Once aboard the *Four Winds* the sailors learn that their ship is actually a blockade runner carrying ammunition to the Confederate Army. Not only does this fact make the journey considerably more dangerous, but an argument ensues among the crew about the morality of aiding the slave owners' cause. Somewhere off the coast of Charleston the crazed deckhand goes down to the hold with a lit candle and the ship explodes. Jim, Rolf, and two other sailors sympathetic to the abolitionists find land and work their way north, posing as soldiers in the Confederate Army. Although one youth is killed in the Battle of Bull Run, the other three sailors manage to desert the Confederacy and join the Union Forces. At the Union camp, Jim is recognized as a boy too young to go to war, and he is sent to the District of Columbia where he signs on an American ship, happy to be back at sea, sailing with a just and friendly crew.

Orphans of the Wind presents yet another dramatic example of the way moral decisions may lead a boy into manhood. Again, the parents of birth have left the young man with nothing but his own stamina and good sense. Again, the death of his parents and the cruelty of his guardian frees the protagonist from the ties that usually subsume ideology to personal loyalty. The reader is invited to feel the struggle and triumph that comes with unfettered moral action. Jim chooses his enemies as well as his friends.

But the moral universe displayed in *Orphans of the Wind* is more complex than that evidenced in Haugaard's books for younger readers. Here one encounters several characters who are kind in spite of their politics, decent people living in the Southern states. Religion crosses the line into madness. Misrepresentation of the truth is, in certain instances, justified.

The metaphorical content of *Orphans in the Wind* also helps mark it as a book intended for older readers. Jim is an orphan who in effect is adopted by a small community of sailors. These men identify themselves as orphans, individuals without families who don't even know the others' real names. But by the tale's end Jim realizes that even his wise friend Rolf might have misunderstood the orphan status of the sailor: "We were not 'orphans of the wind'; we were brothers of the earth, and the wind and the sea were our parents" (183).

The book concludes with Jim on the deck of his new ship, thinking about himself as "a real tar."

> The thought pleased me. I looked up at the mast and the little clouds high above it. The world is good, I thought. And it is mine. Mine the whole world, the sea and the wind. (186)

Jim, like the reader, has learned that nature offers gifts to even the most despairing of humans; this is a world of hope. The appeal of *Orphans of the Wind* lies finally in that vision: orphans can find the direction and solace of parents in nature and community.

The English Civil War Novels of Erik Christian Haugaard

Alethea Helbig

Among Erik Christian Haugaard's books are two that have their background in the English Civil War, *Member for Parliament* and its sequel, *Cromwell's Boy*. As do others of Haugaard's novels, the plots involve a sturdy, intelligent protagonist entering his teens, who is separated from his family, falls under the protection of strangers, undergoes harrowing if exciting experiences, and matures credibly into a self-sufficient youth who seems older than his years. These two novels also exhibit other features familiar to Haugaard's writings, sharply realized scenes, loose but careful plotting, understated style with a disturbingly ironic tone, convincingly drawn period, and sharp looks at the social institutions of religion and of war as a mechanism for problem-solving.

Short frame narratives enclose the two linked plots. An aging Boston gentleman, Oliver Cutter, looks back upon and ponders the events of his youth, when at thirteen he serves as messenger for his namesake who later becomes Lord Protector of England and who, according to Oliver, "unleashed powers that will not be easily bound again" (*Member* 7). He hopes "that there are lessons to be learned from it; and if not that, at least I shall entertain..." (6). He tells how, at twelve, after his mother dies, he and his ne'er-do-well, grandiloquent father go off to war and join the rag-tag camp followers of Lord Essex's ill-organized Parliamentary army. Soon separated from his irresponsible parent, he falls in with a cluster of runaway apprentices, a "little army of youngsters [who] had many enemies" (45), and observes the countryside pillaged, towns plundered, a cathedral ravaged, friends die. After the battle of Edgehill, the boys tramp to London, "a town in turmoil" (85), where Oliver and Easy Jack, a youth of about fourteen now his protector, gain employment with a printer of dubious morality, who sends them to smuggle his propaganda into Royalist-held Oxford. Dispatched from there with a message for Cromwell, they encounter considerable excitement, being captured by an unscrupulous farmer and waylaid by highwaymen. Jack is wounded, and Oliver, separated from this protector, too, continues to Cromwell's headquarters.

Oliver in the role of spy provides the narrative drive for the more cohesive second book. Known in the regiment as "Cromwell's boy," Oliver is valuable to the calculating Colonel for two reasons—he can ride well and he is "by nature silent" (*Cromwell's* 4). He participates in the Battle of Gainsborough, which he describes tellingly as "a besieged city . . . much like an abandoned orphan" (14), from which the Parliamentary forces make an orderly retreat—a victory in itself, in Oliver's opinion. After that, he is sent with letters for influential friends of Cromwell to London, then to Royalist Oxford, where he is to identify for a suspicious Cromwell those attending the King-convened Parliament with a view to determining whose loyalties lie where. Committed to his responsibilities, his primary concern shifts, however, to Faith Powers, the ten-year-old daughter of an inn-keeper who had once befriended him and who is now a political prisoner in Oxford Castle awaiting the rack. Lest Faith, for whom Oliver feels romantic stirrings, be used to loosen her father's tongue against the Roundheads, Oliver engineers a dramatic escape from the city, on a stolen horse and by utilizing a fortuitously overheard password, the ironic "the King's duty." A rousing chase over the countryside provides a grand climax and concludes with Oliver in his namesake's arena, presumably to receive not only his protector's approbation but also further orders.

The loose storyline exhibits conventions of the picaresque and spy-chase genres and therefore offers a full measure of high excitement. Because of its nature, however, the story is less memorable than characters and scenes. Distanced from the reader by the ironic tone and bleak and tumultuous atmosphere, a quiet observer and ruminator by disposition, Oliver is not a protagonist to whom one warms, though one admires his courage and perseverance. Priggish and self-righteous at first, he readily condemns his bombastic father for his weakness for liquor, his need for an audience for his anti-Catholic mouthings, his self-delusion, his irresponsibility. Yet Oliver himself exhibits similar characteristics, and sometimes he recognizes them. He is honest enough to admit that it is not from filial duty alone that he accompanies his father, but for the sheer "desire to go a-soldiering" (*Member* 24), for the prospect of adventure, to be where the action is. Even at the second book's end, it is not out of loyalty to the cause that Oliver stays with Cromwell, but for the glamor of the conflict and the desire to be part of potentially important happenings: he admits he's a "peacock" and enjoys the strutting. He dissembles, and he lies. He is noblest when he transfers the loyalty his dying mother enjoined upon him toward his father to young Faith.

More acted upon than acting, Oliver is a shallow sort who introduces the reader to other ambivalently interesting characters, who together constitute a carefully orchestrated potpourri of the period: Easy Jack, the flamboyant, eloquent, runaway son of a Cavalier-sympathizing Oxford vicar, also in search of adventure; his foil, small, wrinkled, pockmarked Ezra, runaway London apprentice, who has "many dreams and in none of them was he poor" (*Member* 63), just one of many who prey upon those who are weak and who are themselves preyed upon by both foe and partisans; Master Waldon, the unscrupulous, prevaricating printer of London, whose mad, popish daughter, Antonia, becomes an innocent sacrifice to the dubious cause of anti-popery; the Parliament-sympathizing tailor of Oxford so enamored with spying that he lies for the sake of lying and entangles those he seeks to protect; Cromwell, who appears genuinely interested in Oliver because the boy calls up memories of his own dead son but whose mind is primarily on his cause; the sharp-eyed vicar of Brill's wife, who cares for wounded Jack and who deliberately eavesdrops on the boys, simply because she feels adults are morally obligated to keep tabs on boys any way they can. These are just a few of the large and ironically ambivalent cast among whom Oliver wends his precarious way.

If Oliver himself lacks memorability, he functions effectively as a window to the period. Page after page reveals a southeastern England seemingly gone mad, with, from Oliver's vantage at any rate, no clear reasons for the uproar.

There are vivid battle scenes, like that at Edgehill:

> Suddenly, from being spectators, we were in the midst of the battle—if such it could be called and "slaughter" was not a better word.

Jack grabbed my hand and together we ran. The air was filled with sounds: the cries of the wounded and the dying, the horses' hooves as they thundered against the turf, the curses of the defeated, and the shouts of the victorious. . . .
Seeing only the blades of grass at our feet, we waited for the battle to pass us by. (*Member* 66-67)

Oliver sees the Puritans wantonly sack Worcester:

I remember a fat soldier stamping on a crucifix, and when he could not break it, he wedged the wooden cross between two stones and jumped on it.
There were officers who tried to retain some discipline, but it was impossible. The well-ordered town of Worcester that night resembled a house of Bedlam where all the madmen had broken loose. (*Member* 30-31)

He observes hypocrisy and ambivalence:

"Now, Oliver," my father began . . . "If we should take a bit of clothing or sovereign or two, it would not be a sin. We are poor, and those who kiss the pope's toe are rich."
"Are the Catholics not Christian?" I asked . . .
"They have broken God's Laws! What saith the Lord's Second Commandment? . . . But we shall cleanse them of their popish vanity!"
I looked away. I did not bother to argue . . . It was not the idea of looting that repelled me, but his wish to have the Lord's approval of his knavery. (*Member* 29-30)

Civilians exhibit zeal approaching madness, too:

"This is not a Temple of Learning." The Puritan gentleman put his hand on my shoulder. "It is a court of pleasure and vanity! Here the Antichrist reigns! But a Day of Judgment shall come. . . . " As he spoke, a thin smile spread across his face, which made it look cruel.
Faith had taken hold of my hand. Now she dragged me away. "That is what the devil looks like," She declared. . . . (*Member* 123)

Oliver's pithy and sententious manner of speaking underscores the irony:

> It seemed that Colonel Mosley liked to sharpen his wits on his subordinates, and they always make convenient but poor grindstones. (*Cromwell's* 199)
> "The high and mighty never ask what they trample down... The world is the anvil, and they are the hammer, and we are in between, getting all the blows," [comments the blacksmith]. (*Cromwell's* 206-207)
> Yet the dead are easier to bear than the wounded, for on those for whom the world has ceased to be, you can turn your back and walk away. But the wounded will not let you go... for you are their link with life. (*Member* 68)

And the reader is left to ponder the value of the conflict, of any such conflict.

A more attractive figure than Oliver the youth, Oliver the time-tempered adult suggests that that old war was but one of many efforts in the long struggle for human rights. He says that the rabble now "must be added when the mighty do their accounting..." (*Member* 7). At the very last, he says, "no story ever ends"(*Cromwell's* 213), and informs the reader that, because his colony of Massachusetts has lost its charter, he has borrowed a horse and galloped to Connecticut to urge the colonials there to "save their charter from Andros' claws" (*Cromwell's* 214). That recent ride, he remarks, "brought back sweet memories of all my rides in England and the boy I once was... [I] have kept faith with the boy... And what more or what better can an old man do?" (*Cromwell's* 214). The young Oliver played an important role, though he was mostly unaware of its significance. The elderly Oliver sees what he did then and has just done as part of the universal struggle for human dignity. Thus Oliver Cutter ends his book on a hopeful note, with a powerful affirmation of the indomitability of the human spirit.

Erik Haugaard is a fine writer, whose historical fiction in particular, I believe, has not received the attention it deserves. He is a master at creating not only the appearance but also the ethic of a period. His books are excellent adventure stories that also convey important insights into human nature. Moreover, they leave the reader with deep appreciation for the pleasure that skillful use of language brings.

The 1989 Phoenix Award Winner

The Night Watchmen

Helen Cresswell

Bored and lonely Henry, about ten, encounters in the park two middleaged tramps, amiable Josh and his gloomy brother, Caleb, "do-as-you-pleasers" on the watch for mysterious night villains called Greeneyes. When their enemies become too threatening, Henry helps his friends board the night train to "There" and safety. An inventive concept, original characters, careful pacing, escalating tension, and judiciously used humor create an exceptionally entertaining and convincing fantasy.

Acceptance: 1989 Phoenix Award

Helen Cresswell

I was delighted when I heard that *The Night Watchmen* had been given the Phoenix Award, not so much for my own sake—for Josh and Caleb's. This pair have a very special place in my affections. It can be very irritating to an author when a friend, having read one's latest book, says how much he has enjoyed it, then adds—"But I think I still like So and So best"—naming some title written years before. But when that title is *The Night Watchmen*, I make allowances. I have a sneaking sympathy.

You might like to know something of how this book came to be written. The initial idea came simply enough. At that time we lived on a road that was built up on one side only, facing open fields. One day a red and white striped workman's hut went up on the lane. At first I gave it hardly a glance. But day after day it was still there and no real work seemed to be going on. There was just a large hole in the road and a sign—Danger. That was when the idea occurred to me that anyone could put up such a hut, and camp there indefinitely, if they made it look convincing enough. The Electricity people would think it was the Water Board, the Water Board would think it was the Gas Board, the Gas Board . . . and so on. As long as there was a hole in the road you could do it practically anywhere—except, perhaps, outside 10 Downing Street. As Josh says, "You could dig one outside the Houses of Parliament, if you'd a mind to, and as long as nobody fell in it, there'd be no questions asked."

So there was the original idea. I was young then, I had not learned to resist the temptation to start writing in the first excitement of an inspiration. So I sat straight down and the very first names that came into my head were Josh and Caleb, and I knew they were perfect, but didn't know why. At around Chapter 3 the flow stopped dead in its tracks. "Now what?" I wondered. I had exhausted the theme already, it seemed. The night watchmen had set up camp and dug their illicit hole and there was nowhere for the story to go.

I abandoned it. I pushed the exercise book into an old oak corner cupboard I used as a filing cabinet, and forgot all about it. Then, perhaps a year later, I opened the cupboard door and didn't quite manage to slam it shut quickly enough and everything slid out onto the floor. I sighed and set about the long overdue task of tidying it out.

I found the exercise book with those first few thousand words and read them as though they were entirely new to me.

"I *like* these two old boys," I thought. "I'm going to do something with them."

And then the story unfolded, almost, it seemed, of its own accord. When the Greeneyes appeared without warning I became frightened. They seemed so menacing that I would not write the book during the dark evenings if I were alone in the house.

"A grown woman, scared of her own stories!" my husband said.

The book was finished quite quickly. I typed it out and sent it to Faber and Faber. Then, the day after I'd posted it off I sat down and read it through and it seemed to me that there was still an awful menace about it; it scared me. I decided that it was to do with Caleb's name.

"If he had a nice wholesome name like Bill," I thought, "it would make everything all right."

I rang Phyllis Hunt, my editor at Faber. "Look," I said. "I've just sent you a story."

"I know. We've read it—we like it and want to do it."

"There's just one thing," I said. "I've decided I don't like the name Caleb. It's sinister."

She sounded surprised. She had thought it perfect, she said. I persisted.

"I want to change it to Bill. If you could get someone to go through the typescript and change the Calebs to Bills, I'll do the same with my copy."

Reluctantly she agreed. I went and struck out every Caleb and replaced it with a Bill and felt much better.

About a week later I thought I'd read the book through again, confident that all would now be well. I had hardly finished the third chapter when I knew that I had made a terrible mistake. You cannot, you simply cannot change a Caleb into a Bill.

I went and rang Phyllis Hunt. "You remember I asked you to change all the Calebs to Bills?" I asked. "Don't worry. It's been done." I drew a deep breath. "Well, I wonder, would it be an awful bother—could you change them back to Caleb, please? "
There is a very simple lesson here. That names are *vital,* that in a curious way the name *is* the character. (Try changing Peter Pan's first name to Albert.) But there's another interesting thing about this particular case. Years later someone said to me what an excellent idea it had been to take the names Josh and Caleb from the Biblical story. I replied politely that I did not know what he was talking about. Nor did I—consciously. But I looked up the references, and could see that my subconscious had stored those names from childhood, when we read the story at school. And I could see why, when those names sprang unbidden into my head, I knew that they were perfect.

A psychologist once told me that the Night Watchmen and the secret place they inhabit—There—represent the creative imagination. I now think it very likely that this is true, though at the time I simply thought I was telling a story. At the time I wrote this book there was a great vogue for so called "social realism" in children's books. My own work was amongst others under attack as being "unrealistic" and "escapist." I felt threatened, just as Josh and Caleb are threatened by the Greeneyes. And the reason I loved them so much and love them still is that the Night Watchmen are free wheeling, what Russell Hoban called "self winding," and fiercely guarding their right to be so.

Another strange thing. I had no idea when I hit on the idea of Greeneyes to represent menace, why I did so. Again, years later my husband and I were discussing nightmares, and especially recurrent nightmares we had as children. I started to recount one which I had so often that even after it had begun I would try to fight my way out, knowing what inevitably would follow. In this dream I would be walking alone, as a very small child, down a long, wide straight road that I walked every day to school. There was a crossroads, at a place known as The Three Lamps. On the corner was a gloomy old house with a high stone wall. I would see an opening in this wall, with steps leading downwards into the darkness. I had this dream so often that I would fight against the strong compulsion to descend those stone steps. Down I would go, and as I went I would hear a heavy clang, and a heavy door swung shut to close the opening behind me and shut out the light. I found myself in a huge cavern, and looking fearfully about me, straining into the darkness I saw—there in the corner—a pair of green eyes.

It was only in the moment of retelling this nightmare that I recalled it. Now I knew why the Greeneyes held such terror for me, even in the writing.

So that is how *The Night Watchmen* came into being, triggered partly by one simple idea, but eventually drawing on who knows what hidden sources and emotions.

This book taught me a great deal and more than any book I have ever written taught me to trust the secret and unpredictable workings of the subconscious mind. If you trust it—and it takes some nerve to do so—it will not fail you. That oak cupboard into which I shut those first three chapters was, in effect, my own subconscious. I've often felt tempted since, when stuck, to shut things up in there again—as if it had magic powers and would write my books for me if I left them in there long enough. The trouble is, it wouldn't then *be* subconscious!

It now remains to thank you all for bestowing on *The Night Watchmen* the high honor of the Phoenix Award. I am sorry that I cannot be with you to do so personally. Any friends of Josh and Caleb are friends of mine. And if they survive another twenty years, or longer, it will be due in part to this recognition. I thank you.

Helen Cresswell

Since her first book, the illustrated story *Sonya-by-the-Shore,* came out in 1960, British author Helen Cresswell has published more than seventy novels, short stories in illustrated form, plays, television scripts, and readers, a wide variety of writing almost entirely for children and young adults. This amazingly prolific output has earned her high praise from critics and reviewers as being among the most exciting, unpredictable, and entertaining of contemporary authors for young readers. Most acclaimed for her fantasy novels, Cresswell's efforts in that genre have ranged from the tall tale to the comic to the macabre, with stories of magic and the supernatural besides. All are related with zest and good humor and amply demonstrate that a lively and inventive mind created them.

Cresswell began writing at an early age, both prose and poetry, and continued throughout her teens, the experimentation with form and technique she did at that time resulting in the inventiveness evident later in her work as an adult. When she was sixteen, she received the Nottinghamshire Poetry Society Award for best poem, initiating the trend for winning awards she has maintained since, most notably for her novels.

Among the most prestigious of these prizes is the Phoenix Award, which she received for *The Night Watchmen,* the first time this award was given for a book of fantasy. *The Night Watchmen* was also commended for the Carnegie Award, as were the fantasies *Up the Pier* and *The Bongleweed.* The former is a time-travel story in which a family from the past finds itself on a lonely pier in a small Welsh seacoast town. A comic tale, *The Bongleweed* takes astonishing liberties with natural science in telling about giant tropical plants with dense, entangling foliage that begin engulfing a neighborhood.

The Bongleweed was named to their Fanfare list of notable books by the editors of *The Horn Book Magazine,* as was *The Winter of the Birds.* Sober in comparison to these other books, *The Winter of the*

Birds examines the nature of heroism when a boy and an old man combat some terrible steel birds that flock in their part of town.

Selected for the *Choice* list of books for academic libraries, as well as being nominated for the Carnegie award, is *The Piemakers,* one of Cresswell's early fantasies and still among her most entertaining. This novel marked a distinct jumping-off point in her career as a writer of humorous fantasies and set the tone for her later work. It celebrates a recurring theme in her books, that of pride in craftsmanship, as it tells tongue-in-cheek about the outrageous, yet completely believable in context, adventures of a gifted family of pie bakers.

Ordinary Jack, also cited in *Choice,* initiated a series of realistic novels that have become immensely popular. Jack is the much-derided younger son in a large and talented family of overachievers. Their efforts to draw attention to themselves and prove their uniqueness, combined with Jack's attempts to elevate himself in their esteem, result in many uproarious situation comedy scenes.

Several of Cresswell's books have been chosen as Notable Children's Books by the American Library Association and some as Children's Books of the Year by the Child Study Children's Book Committee. One, *The Secret World of Polly Flint,* was runner-up for the Whitbread Award.

Cresswell was born in Nottinghamshire, England, in 1934, the daughter of an electrical engineer. She attended Nottinghamshire Girls' High School and received her B.A. with honors in English from King's College, University of London. She held positions as a literary assistant to the author of a book on Van Gogh, writer for the television arm of the British Broadcasting Corporation, teacher, and fashion buyer. She married Brian Rowe, who has been employed in textiles, has two daughters, and has made her home in a 200-year-old farmhouse on a hill at the edge of Robin Hood's Sherwood Forest, a site that seems fitting indeed for a writer who has contributed so much to the literary enjoyment of today's children.

Books by Helen Cresswell

Sonya-by-the-Shore. Illus. Robin Jane Wells. London: Dent, 1960.
Jumbo Spencer. Illus. Clixby Watson. Leicester: Brockhampton, 1963; Philadelphia: Lippincott, 1966.
The White Sea Horse. Illus. Robin Jacques. Edinburgh: Oliver and Boyd, 1964; Philadelphia: Lippincott, 1965.
Jumbo Back to Nature. Illus. Leslie Wood. Leicester: Brockhampton, 1965.
Pietro and the Mule. Illus. Maureen Eckersley. Edinburgh: Oliver and Boyd, 1965; Indianapolis: Bobbs Merrill, 1965.
Jumbo Afloat. Illus. Leslie Wood. Leicester: Brockhampton, 1966.
Where the Wind Blows. Illus. Peggy Fortnum. London: Faber, 1966; New York: Funk and Wagnalls, 1968.
The Piemakers. Illus. V. H. Drummond. London: Faber, 1967; Philadelphia: Lippincott, 1968.
A Day on Big O. Illus. Shirley Hughes. London: Benn, 1967; Chicago: Follett, 1968.
A Tide for the Captain. Illus. Robin Jacques. Edinburgh: Oliver and Boyd, 1967.
The Signposters. Illus. Gareth Floyd. London: Faber, 1968.
Jumbo and the Big Dig. Illus. Leslie Wood. Leicester: Brockhampton, 1968.
The Barge Children. Illus. Lynette Hemmant. London: Hodder and Stoughton, 1968.
The Sea Piper. Illus. Robin Jacques. Edinburgh: Oliver and Boyd, 1968.
Rug Is a Bear. Illus. Susanna Gretz. London: Benn, 1968.
Rug Plays Tricks. Illus. Susanna Gretz. London: Benn, 1968.
Rug Plays Ball. Illus. Susanna Gretz. London: Benn, 1969.
Rug and a Picnic. Illus. Susanna Gretz. London: Benn, 1969.
The Night Watchmen. Illus. Gareth Floyd. London: Faber, 1969; New York: Macmillan, 1969; Aladdin, 1989.

A Gift from Winklesea. Illus. Janina Ede. Leicester: Brockhampton, 1969.
A Game of Catch. Illus. Gareth Floyd. London: Chatto, 1969; New York, Macmillan, 1977.
A House for Jones. Illus. Margaret Gordon. London: Benn, 1969.
The Outlanders. Illus. Doreen Roberts. London: Faber, 1970.
Rainbow Pavement. Illus. Shirley Hughes. London: Benn, 1970.
The Wilkses. Illus. Gareth Floyd. London: BBC, 1970; as *Time Out.* Cambridge: Lutterworth, 1987; New York: Macmillan, 1990.
John's First Fish. Illus. Prudence Seward. London: Macmillan, 1970.
At the Stroke of Midnight: Traditional Fairy Tales Retold. Illus. Carolyn Dinan. London: Collins, 1971.
The Bird Fancier. Illus. Renate Meyer. London: Benn, 1971.
Up the Pier. Illus. Gareth Floyd. London: Faber, 1971; New York: Macmillan, 1972.
The Weather Cat. Illus. Margery Gill. London: Benn, 1971.
The Beachcombers. Illus. Errol Le Cain. London: Faber, 1972; New York: Macmillan, 1972.
Bluebirds over Pit Row. Illus. Richard Kennedy. London: Benn, 1972.
Jane's Policeman. Illus. Margery Gill. London: Benn, 1972.
The Long Day. Illus. Margery Gill. London: Benn, 1972.
Roof Fall! Illus. Richard Kennedy. London: Benn, 1972.
Short Back and Sides. Illus. Richard Kennedy. London: Benn, 1972.
The Beetle Hunt. Illus. Anne Knight. London: Longman, 1973.
The Bongleweed. Illus. Ann Strugnell. London: Faber, 1973; New York: Macmillan, 1974.
The Bower Birds. Illus. Margery Gill. London; Benn, 1973.
The Key. Illus. Richard Kennedy. London: Benn, 1973.
Lizzie Dripping. Illus. Jenny Thorne. London: BBC, 1973.
Lizzie Dripping by the Sea. Illus. Faith Jaques. London: BBC, 1974.
Lizzie Dripping and the Little Angel. Illus. Faith Jaques. London: BBC, 1974.
Lizzie Dripping Again. Illus. Faith Jaques. London: BBC, 1974.
Two Hoots. Illus. Martine Blanc. London: Benn, 6 vols., 1974-77; New York: Crown, 6 vols., 1978.
More Lizzie Dripping. Illus. Faith Jaques. London: BBC, 1974.
Cheap Day Return. Illus. Richard Kennedy. London: Benn, 1974.
Shady Deal. Illus. Richard Kennedy. London: Benn, 1974.
The Trap. Illus. Richard Kennedy. London: Benn, 1974.

Butterfly Chase. Illus. Margery Gill. London: Kestrel, 1975.
The Winter of the Birds. London: Faber, 1975; New York: Macmillan, 1976.
The Bagthorpe Saga. Illus. by Jill Bennett. All published by London: Faber, and New York: Macmillan.
  Ordinary Jack. 1977.
  Absolute Zero. 1978.
  Bagthorpes Unlimited. 1978.
  Bagthorpes v. the World. 1979
  Bagthorpes Abroad. 1984
  Bagthorpes Haunted. 1985.
  Bagthorpes Liberated. 1989.
Donkey Days. Illus. Shirley Hughes. London: Benn, 1977.
Awful Jack. Illus. Joanna Stubbs. London: Hodder and Stoughton, 1977.
The Flyaway Kite. Illus. Bridget Clarke. London: Kestrel, 1979.
My Aunt Polly by the Sea. Illus. Margaret Gordon. Exeter: Wheaton, 1980.
Nearly Goodbye. Illus. Tony Morris. London: Macmillan, 1980.
Penny for the Guy. Illus. Nicole Goodwin. London: Macmillan, 1980.
Dear Shrink. London: Faber, 1982; New York: Macmillan, 1982.
The Secret World of Polly Flint. Illus. Shirley Felts. London: Faber, 1982; New York: Macmillan, 1984.
Ellie and the Hagwitch. Illus. Jonathan Heap. London: Hardy, 1984.
Petticoat Smuggler. Illus. Shirley Bellwood. London: Macmillan, 1985.
Greedy Alice. Illus. Martin Honeysett. London: Deutsch, 1986.
Whodunnit? Illus. Caroline Browne. London: Cape, 1986.
Dragon Ride. Illus. Liz Roberts. London: Kestrel, 1987.
Moondial. London: Faber, 1987; New York: Macmillan, 1987.
Trouble. Illus. Margaret Chamberlain. London: Gollancz, 1987; New York: Dutton, 1988.
The Story of Grace Darling. Illus. Paul Wright. London: Viking, 1988.
Rosie and the Boredom Eater. London: Heineman, 1989.
Hokey Pokey Did It! Loughborough: Ladybird, 1989.
Almost Goodbye Guzzler. Illus. Judy Brown. London: Blackie, 1990.

Meet Posy Bates. Illus. Kate Aldous. London: Bodley Head, 1990; New York: Macmillan, 1992.
Posy Bates Again! London: Bodley Head, 1991.

Magic at the Edges:
An Appreciation of *The Night Watchmen*

Mark I. West

A lifelong resident of Nottinghamshire, England, Helen Cresswell lives in an old farmhouse on the fringes of Sherwood Forest, the same forest where Robin Hood and Little John are said to have hidden during the reign of King Richard I. Although Cresswell wrote *The Night Watchmen* nearly eight centuries after the time of Robin Hood, something of his spirit seems to have made its way into the book. Like Robin Hood, Josh and Caleb, the title characters in *The Night Watchmen*, are larger than life, full of mystery and power. Like Robin Hood, they exist outside the bounds of respectable society but are frequent visitors to it. And, like Robin Hood, they successfully elude enemies, enjoy life's simple pleasures, and befriend the weak.

In Cresswell's story, the weak are represented by Henry, a boy of about ten who is recuperating from a lengthy illness. He is feeling somewhat better when the story opens, but his doctor recommends that he stay home from school for another month. He is not permitted to do anything strenuous, but he is allowed to wander around Mandover, the English town where he lives. One morning, while walking through the park, he meets two tramps, or so he assumes. He is immediately attracted to Josh, who is jovial and kindhearted, but he is not so sure about Caleb, who seems rather cross to Henry. Still, he is fascinated by the air of secrecy that surrounds the tramps and is determined to find out more about them.

Josh and Caleb gradually let Henry into their lives, allowing him to participate in their activities and entrusting him with some of their secrets. Henry learns that they travel from town to town so that Josh can conduct research for a book he is writing about places. Disguised as workmen, they dig a deep hole which they carefully mark with a sign that reads "Danger Men at Work." They then erect a portable hut near the hole and go about their business. For Josh, this consists of touring local landmarks, interviewing town officials, and exploring out-of-the-way neighborhoods. For Caleb, it consists of preparing gourmet meals and keeping an eye on Josh. As they explain to Henry, they are "do-as-you-pleasers," and they do just that.

In some ways, Josh and Caleb seem like a pair of amusing hoboes, but Henry soon discovers that their peculiarities go beyond the mere eccentric. For one thing, they have an obsession with trains, especially one that they call the night train. This is no ordinary train. Not only does it run at night, but it answers to Josh and Caleb's call. As Josh puts it, "She comes to our whistle the long and broad of England. She can weave her way through the junctions like a homing pigeon. . . . She's a rare, secret one she is" (46).

Exactly where Josh and Caleb go when they ride the night train is never clear, but their destination does not strike Henry as the sort of place one could find on a map.

Another strange thing that Henry learns about Josh and Caleb is that they are being pursued by dangerous enemies. These enemies look like ordinary people except that they have bright green eyes. More than anything else, the Greeneyes want to ride the night train, and they are determined to learn the secret whistle that Josh and Caleb use to summon the train. Eluding the Greeneyes is no easy job. Even when they are relaxing in the safety of their hut, Josh and Caleb have to be on their guard, for a Greeneye might be hiding in the shadows.

Although Josh and Caleb are appealing characters, the success of the book has a lot to do with Cresswell's carefully paced and inventive plot. Like a fine mystery writer, Cresswell does not divulge all her characters' secrets at once. Nor does she spell out all the book's fantasy elements. For much of the book, we are not sure if Josh and Caleb are mad or magical. We are not even certain if the night train really exists or if the Greeneyes are real enemies. Even at the close of the book, we are still left with questions about Josh and Caleb and their ultimate destination.

Cresswell keeps the magic at the edges of her story, but she succeeds in creating a world that is just as wondrous as the worlds in more overt works of fantasy. In his preface to *The Merry Adventures of Robin Hood*, Howard Pyle made a similar observation about Robin Hood's world. "This country," he wrote, "is not Fairy-land. What is it? 'Tis the land of Fancy." I cannot think of a better way to describe the world of *The Night Watchmen*.

The Bagthorpe Saga of Helen Cresswell, or What Happens When Eccentricity Becomes the Norm

Millicent Lenz

Helen Cresswell first introduced the Bagthorpes, a family of English eccentrics, in her 1977 novel, *Ordinary Jack*. Ordinary Jack Matthew Bagthorpe, "with an *e*," as he insists, is eleven years old and suffers from being the only "ordinary" human being in his extraordinary clan. Feeling a need to distinguish himself and urged on by his Uncle Parker, Jack indulges in a scheme to establish his credentials as a "prophet." He becomes ego-involved with his dog, Absolute Zero, with whom he identifies for their shared inferiority-complex. Absolute Zero has been ridiculed by Mr. Bagthorpe as a "mutton-headed and pudding-footed mongrel" ever since his unexplained appearance in the Bagthorpes' garden. It was Mr. Bagthorpe who gave the lacklustre hound his name, declaring that "If there was anything less than nothing . . . that hound would be it" (*OJ* 19).

The initial volume of the Saga also introduces the reader to the other key players. There are the three other Bagthorpe children, Rosie, the younger sister, who excels in swimming and painting; Tess, the older sister, a devotee of science and the occult; William, the elder brother, a specialist in electronics who talks via ham radio with Anonymous from Grimsby, who claims to be a pirate. William basks in the reflected romantic glow of his pirate friend. The father of these *wunderkinder*, Henry Bagthorpe, writes television scripts, and the mother, Laura, is both a justice of the peace and the author of an Ann Landers-type advice column under the pseudonym of Stella Bright.

Dwelling with the Bagthorpes are Grandma and Grandpa, the former a spirited old crone who is obsessed with the memory of her "sainted" dead cat, Thomas, and who likes nothing better than setting off a row, the latter a meek old gentleman whose "selective" deafness insulates him from the pandemonium that often erupts around him.

But this is not all. The extended Bagthorpe clan includes Aunt Celia, a fabulously beautiful and "poetic" creature who lives with her idle and rich husband, "Uncle" Parker, not far away, and their darling daughter, the five-year-old Unholy Terror, Daisy, a child given to pyromania, among other destructive antics. Uncle Parker is regarded as an unredeemed villain by Grandma, because it was his notoriously wild driving of an expensive motorcar that caused Thomas's untimely death. He is regarded with a mixture of envy and disdain by Henry Bagthorpe, who has to work for a living, whereas Uncle Parker only plays around with stocks and shares for about an hour each morning. Uncle Parker, moreover, infuriates others by continuing to look lean and fit even though he does little more than lounge around sipping gin and toying with crossword puzzles.

There is also "Fozzy," Mrs. Fosdyke, the Bagthorpes' long-suffering housekeeper, who tolerates the zany crew (though she wisely refuses to "sleep in"); she finds them useful to her own purposes because they appreciate her culinary talents, on which she prides herself, and they provide her with colorful stories to entertain her cronies at the local pub, where she takes her daily pint. A practical, prosaic woman, she serves along with Jack and Absolute Zero as a foil for the farcical "genius" characters who belong to Northrop Frye's *alazon,* or "imposter," type. Jack and Zero and Mrs. Fosdyke are the fixed stars by whom the reader can navigate through the stormy shoals generated by the more mercurial Bagthorpes.

I shall sketch what I believe to be Cresswell's chief strengths as a writer, by reference to certain features of the Saga. First, she excels in creating farcical situations that stem from the characters' deficient self-knowledge and resulting self-aggrandizement. An obvious example can be drawn from *Ordinary Jack,* when eleven-year-old ordinary Jack, in his "prophet" guise, fakes mysterious visions, and his acting succeeds remarkably for a time. However, he makes the mistake of recording the entire fiendish plot in a journal, which his father uncovers when he surreptitiously raids Jack's stack of comics. Both the father and Jack are exposed as frauds, amidst much hilarity. The elder Bagthorpe suffers more from the unmasking, because he has falsely ridiculed the reading of comics as beneath him, and must now admit to puffery. The hot air balloon, or Great Bubble, that plays a part in the debacle of the final scene, can be seen as a metaphor of what Uncle Parker calls the Bagthorpes' "exhibitionism" (*OJ* 9).

One more example of the many farcical situations will be mentioned. In *Bagthorpes Unlimited: Being the Third Part of the Bagthorpe Saga*, Grandma reads of a way to burglar-proof one's house during one's absence by leaving a note and twenty pounds in easy sight of any intruder, telling the wretch that "There is nothing of any real value in this house, so please do not ransack it. Please take twenty pounds with my compliments" (*BU* 7).

Impressed as she is with this idea, Grandma is loathe to part with twenty pounds, and substitutes her brilliant idea: a note listing the most valued items in the household, together with the request, phrased with the utmost courtesy, that the burglar *not* take the specified valuable items. When a burglar actually appears on the scene, he has a ready-made guide to the valuables and naturally ransacks everything on the list. However, there is a further twist: the stolen items prove disgusting to the burglar (they are chiefly sentimental treasures), who subsequently abandons them at the wicket gate, together with his note that they are "rubbish," and claiming that was "a dirty trick to stoop to." All of this is highly publicized (the Bagthorpes now being television celebrities), and the family becomes the laughingstock of England.

Cresswell's second achievement in this Saga is her handling of an unarticulated deep comic irony. Superficially, eccentricity is linked with creativity; at least this idea is verbally expressed. For instance, Aunt Celia says, in apologizing for Daisy's outlandish, pyromanical behavior, that she is "creative" (*BU* 17). To this, Henry Bagthorpe replies, "There is no such thing as destructive creativity." On the surface, going to extremes is linked with genius, as in this description of Jack's limitations: "Jack's unwillingness to go to extremes was one of the things that marked him as irreversibly ordinary, and that ruled out his ever being a genius. He was totally lacking in the necessary ruthlessness and obsessiveness that characterized his siblings" (*BU* 46). The family's motto, we are told, if they had one, would be "Enough is not Enough," or "Too Much if Never Enough," or as Mr. Bagthorpe suggests, "If a Thing's Worth Doing, It's Worth Overdoing" (*BU* 47). In *Bagthorpes Abroad*, Henry Bagthorpe expands upon his theory that creativity is linked to unpredictability and wild swings of mood when he describes "all great creative artists" as manic-depressive (*BA* 110). He is of course excusing his own erratic tendencies.

If one reads beneath the surface a very different meaning emerges, never voiced. In contrast to the paranoia-inducing, self-described "brilliance" of the other Bagthorpes, which prevents them from inspiring warm and friendly feelings (*BU* 106), Jack is capable of "empathy with the plight of others." Unlike them, he is not "pure ego" (*BA* 108). It is notable that only Jack has the "genius" to bring along the camping-out gear that makes it possible for the family to prepare a meal in the haunted mansion they take for their holiday in Wales (*BA* 63). It is the steady, "ordinary" Jack who after all succeeds in teaching the even more ordinary Absolute Zero to fetch, by the novel method of going on his hands and knees to model the process for him (*OJ*). Ironically, where the bombastic geniuses outnumber the ordinary, the ordinary become rare. In the country where imposters are the majority, the regular, straightforward Jack and his common, somewhat dull mutt are refreshingly different, and their innovations are at least not destructive. One should not forget that it is the very diffidence and nonchalance of Absolute Zero that captivate the television director who makes the canine a star: Zero's "resigned, world-weary" way of crunching on his dog food and his refusal to get excited, much less to go to extremes, make him the ultimate television star. It is finally the understated, enduring, self-deprecating qualities of both Jack and Absolute Zero that are creative in the sense of making modest growth of character possible. They qualify in this sense as examples of Frye's *eiron* character, who balances and finally deflates the excesses of the *alazon*.

Cresswell's third achievement, and possibly her greatest, is her deft use of language, and a resultant wit and verbal zest. She can turn a phrase splendidly, as with Uncle Parker's winning slogan in the Sugar-coated Puffball breakfast cereal contest: "Get tough with Sugar-Puff" (*AZ* 25). She can also be pleasingly clever in her metaphors, as when the self-indulgent foibles of Great Aunt Lucy are put into perspective by the narrator's comment, "The Bees in her Bonnet had always been kept slavishly supplied with nectar by those around her" (*BW* 76). Cresswell herself has testified to her "passion for words as *words*" and this passion manifests itself in the verbal richness of her works (Montreville 105).

An overall assessment of the Bagthorpe Saga must give credit to its success as "uproarious situation comedy," in Marcus Crouch's phrase. He considers Cresswell at her best in drawing "eccentrics" (Crouch 206).[1] Her fascination with eccentrics relates, I believe, to her professed interest in "the infinite possibilities of life," "the daily encounter with miracle." She remarks, "I am moved by what Hopkins called 'all things counter, original, spare, strange,' and at the same time by the richness of ordinary lives and ordinary people." (Montreville 105-6).

Fascinated as she is by eccentrics, she sees "miracle" in the commonplace. Her own words best illuminate her accomplishment in the Bagthorpe Saga, which by deflating human pretensions, calls forth the laughter and wonder to be found in the ordinary, and manifests a truly inclusive comic perspective, revelling in both the strangeness and the mundanity of life.

Note

1. Crouch also comments that the "cult" fostered by the television series has been "good for sales but not so good for creativity." A number of book reviewers have found the comedy of the later books in the Saga, particularly those set in Wales, to be rather forced, in contrast to the more natural flow of the initial volumes. In the later novels, a narrative difficulty results from the need to recapitulate some events of the earlier books.

Works Cited

Crouch, Marcus. "Helen Cresswell." *Twentieth Century Children's Writers*. Ed. D. L. Kirkpatrick. New York: St. Martin's, 1983.
Montreville, Doris de and Elizabeth D. Crawford, eds. "Helen Cresswell." *Fourth Book of Junior Authors and Illustrators*. New York: H. W. Wilson, 1978.

Playing with Convention
Four Novels by Helen Cresswell

Alethea Helbig

In addition to *The Night Watchmen* and *Ordinary Jack* of the Bagthorpe series, four other novels by Cresswell have received major critical citations. Among their honors, three were recommended for the Carnegie Award in England. These are, in order of publication, *Up the Pier*, *The Bongleweed*, and *The Winter of the Birds*. The fourth book, *The Piemakers*, was named to the *Horn Book* Fanfare list and included on the list of children's books recommended for an academic library published by *Choice* magazine. Although they range widely in subject matter and approach, they have in common carefully controlled eccentricity and well-molded protagonists who capture the reader's intellectual as well as emotional interest. Their grotesquerie artfully tempered with wit, they mark Cresswell as a daring and innovative writer, one unusually adept at reworking conventions and utilizing form and language in new and fresh ways that result in superior storytelling.

While each has its own special attraction, these four novels are not equally successful, though one must always applaud Cresswell's bold invention. In *The Bongleweed*, she capitalizes on moral ambivalency in such a way that the reader derives a perverse pleasure from sly Becky's spying on her parents' employers through a tiny hole in their common livingroom wall, and even from the way Becky sets up for trouble the posh young relative who has come to stay with the employers by telling him to plant seeds that she knows have potential for remarkable growth. She does indeed have to confront the fruits of her deception, in the form of an exotic tropical plant that thrives in spite of repeated uprootings, vines over the local cemetery, and finally even ramps over the church building, completely covering it and its tower besides. That such a life-loving plant, obviously magical, should in the end succumb to the first frost of fall does not quite convince, however. The book remains, nevertheless, a striking affirmation of the wonder of growing things and of the ordering power of nature.

The Winter of the Birds doesn't quite come out right either. This essentially sober story brings together an unlikely and intriguing mix of characters—a thwarted suicide and his astonishing savior, a highly assured, red-haired Irishman of many words and huge body; a lady grocer of strongly held, readily voiced convictions; an old, half-mad recluse, who is the butt of neighborhood jokes and is convinced of the reality of destructive steel birds; and young Edward Flack, who longs to be a hero, dares himself to do brave deeds, and ruminates on the nature of heroism. But the book has a complicated structure, combining different points of view and linear narrative with diary and letters. The reader doubts the reality of the birds as interest shifts to the examination of heroism and the question of the identity of the Irishman. The theme, however, that true heroism lies in doing whatever one must do, even if everyone else is against it, comes through strongly.

In *Up the Pier*, the reader is also left somewhat in doubt about how much of the story really happened and how much comes from the protagonist's lively imagination and inner psychological needs. On an old, almost abandoned fog-shrouded pier in a Welsh seaside town, lonely Carrie encounters the Pontifexes, a family whose magician grandfather's spell has gone awry and transported them fifty years into the future from their proper year of 1921. For days Carrie rejoices in their company, until she comes to realize that she must sacrifice her own pleasure and wish them back home again for the magic to reverse their situation. The suspense is first-rate, the sober atmosphere lightened with gentle humor, and the eccentricity of the Pontifexes is exploited with kindness.

My favorite of these four books is the earliest published, *The Piemakers*, a story that Marcus Crouch has called the "real foundation-stone of... [Cresswell's] work" (Crouch 206). This lighthearted tall tale focuses on a family that makes and sells pies, mostly meat, but occasionally a fruit one or two, told from the point of view of the only child, a daughter, ten-year-old Gravella Roller, who is always a shrewd observer of the action and sometimes contributes to it.

The first part of the book is devoted to establishing the characters and the importance of piemaking to the family and community. The Rollers live in Danby Dale, England, a pre-Industrial Revolution village of cottage industries. The Rollers include hardworking, conciliatory, red-haired Arthy, the father, and acerbic, status-conscious Jem, the mother, in addition to Gravella. They and their neighbors are skilled at and proud of their work.

"It's in the blood," Arthy often said. "Once a piemaker, always a piemaker. My father was one, my grandfather, my great-grandfather, and for all I know back to Adam and Eve. Whether Adam was one I don't know, but myself I think it very likely."

Jem would sometimes argue about this, saying that it was going too far, but Gravella could see that she was secretly pleased to think that it might be so, and that she was proud of having married into so rich a heritage. (21)

Arthy and Jem can make pies to order, some very large, others ordinary in size, but all perfect in texture of crust and blend of ingredients for the stew. Arthy is responsible for the crust and mixing the filling, Jem for the herbs, and Gravella for the other seasonings. Arthy loves all aspects of the task, starting with the recipes.

There was only one shelf of books in the whole house and that was in the kitchen. Nobody ever read anything but recipe books. They weren't even books, in the strictest sense, because there were very few sentences in them. Most of them were in Arthy's own laborious handwriting and contained lists of ingredients and little marginal notes that only he could understand, like "Sage half and two tbsps and no B," or "Crust half x quarter x four hours."

Often Jem would read one in bed at night if she was having difficulty in dropping off and Gravella would hear her loud whispers as she woke Arthy to explain bits that she couldn't understand, or to share her excitement at some discovery.

"Arthy! Arthy! Wake up! Look! Isn't this the one we made when your Clover married the miller from Fendale? Don't you 'call it, that one where we tried the sultanas and then went and forgot the cinnamon? Oh, I'll never forget that one, not if I live to be a hundred and ten, like grandmother did." (16-17)

All this is related in a light, but never frivolous or satirical tone, and the whimsey strengthens the credibility of the fantasy.

The story falls into two parts, each revolving around the construction of a special pie. The first, commissioned for the King, is Arthy's first ever failure—too much pepper. Jem says this happened because their rival Rollers in Gorby Dale have given them an incorrect version of the King's special recipe. Gravella thinks she may have copied the recipe wrong. At any rate, Arthy falls into a depression. " 'For all the world like a duck without a quack,' as Jem picturesquely put it" (63). . . . 'I think I'm finished with pies,' [Arthy] would say whenever Jem brought the subject up. 'I just haven't got the heart for them any more' "(63).

Then a King's herald comes to town, and the story quickens. There is to be a contest, with a prize of one hundred pounds to whichever village makes the best and biggest pie. The townspeople send a delegation to ask Arthy to enter, to make a pie that would be the biggest ever made—one to feed 2,000 people. Now, pie for twenty is believable. One for 2,000 is truly incredible, but not as Cresswell works it out.

Careful preparations for piemaking begin. The whole village participates, converting Farmer Leary's barn into a bakehouse, assembling the ingredients, the meat, the herbs, vats of water, assigning jobs—all under Arthy's expert supervision, of course. They commission a blacksmith upriver to construct the pie-dish, which they then float down the river disguised as a boat, so Gorby Dale and Cranbock Dale and other villages won't learn how big a pie the Danby Dalers plan.

Suspense comes not from outward tension, like the possibility of sabotage, but over whether or not the other villages will get wind of what the Danby Dalers are doing and over how the Danby people will manage so large a pie. The author works out the details of the construction very carefully.

> Gravella knew that this was the most important moment of all. All the men holding the metal trays had to keep their parts absolutely level with the rest. If one man let his part drop, or lifted it too high, then the pastry would break and the crust be torn. Those great, clumsy Dalesmen, with their thick fingers and booted feet, lifted that crust as if it were glass beaten to snapping thinness. They went towards the pie-dish tiptoe and jaws ajar, staring-eyed, breath

held, slowly, half adread. As the first three men lifted the trays to their shoulders ready to slide them over the top of the dish, Gravella shut her eyes, content to be a coward. There was a slow, soft scraping, a long sigh from the watchers, and Gravella opened her eyes to see the pie capped, looking at last like a real pie, nearly a thousand times larger than life. Arthy, edging round it perched on a ladder, fussing over the edges, looked like Tom Thumb in the giant's pantry. (126-27)

The pie bakes. The contest is held on the meadow near Farmer Leary's barn, because that's the biggest place around and because the king is lodging nearby at the Baron's house. The other villages bring their pies which are admired, and then the cry goes up for the Danby pie, which is majestically wheeled out.

... and the doors of the barn opened slowly on great groaning hinges. There was sudden silence. Out from the shadows came the huge pie-dish, wheeled by twenty men with straining shoulders. The sun fell for the first time on to that glorious crust, perfectly smooth and brown, gleaming faintly. It was impossible, a miracle under that blue sky, standing among the grass and clover like some enormous fruit. It was seen and yet impossible to believe ... For a full minute the pie stood there and more than three thousand people stood and stared in silence, made into statues by their disbelief. Then the roar that broke out sent the skylarks somersaulting skyward and the din broke in deafening fragments and Arthy was borne up into the air and shouldered to the King. (134-36)

The last pages of the story are appropriately devoted to a typical Roller family discussion, a postmortem conversation about proportions and ingredients. It was a spendid pie; could it have been made better? In an epilogue, the author adds a straightfaced comment which enhances the humor. She says that in Danby Dale there exists today on the village green an oblong duck pond that looks much like a pie-dish and is very fact the pie-dish of the story.

This celebration of pride in craftsmanship excels in originality of concept and is in exquisite control of all elements, characterization, pacing, and delineation of setting. Cresswell has said that *The Piemakers* has been her own favorite because she feels it is her "first book in which humour and fantasy became fused" (Commire 64). It certainly does that, and masterfully. It also explores a substantial theme, and does it through just plain good storytelling.

Works Cited

Commire, Anne. *Something about the Author.* Vol. 48. Detroit: Gale Research, 1987.

Crouch, Marcus. "Helen Cresswell." *Twentieth Century Writers for Children.* Ed. D. L. Kirkpatrick. New York: St. Martin's, 1983.

1989 Phoenix Award Honor Book

Brother, Can You Spare a Dime?

Milton Meltzer

Milton Meltzer

By the time he was seventy years old, Milton Meltzer had published about seventy books, almost all of them substantial works of nonfiction, and he has continued to produce outstanding books well into his eighth decade. Among writers of factual books for young people, he is preeminent in his ability to bring social history and the lives of men and women of the past alive to a new generation of readers.

Meltzer was born in 1915, the son of Jewish immigrants, both parents from villages in what was then Austria and more recently has been part of the Soviet Union. In his autobiographical *Starting from Home: A Writer's Beginnings,* he tells of his childhood in Worcester, Massachusetts, where his father was a professional window cleaner and the family lived in spare but not poverty-ridden circumstances, a childhood more like that pictured by Norman Rockwell than the inner-city squalor of most big cities or even the crowded tenement living of the Lower East Side of New York, from which his parents moved before his birth. By the time he was in high school, however, the Great Depression had begun, and he could see its effects in Worcester, where it struck hard as it did in all the industrial areas of the Northeast. Calls for his father's services diminished; his mother's attempts at small business failed. He attended Columbia University on a scholarship, worked as a writer for the WPA Federal Theater Project, and served in the Air Force in World War II.

The difficulties in his own family and in those around him made a deep impression that is reflected not only in *Brother, Can You Spare a Dime?* but also in his interest in minorities, labor movements, peace activists, and women's rights advocates. His first published book, written with Langston Hughes, was *A Pictorial History of the Negro in America,* and he continued to write about African-Americans in *In Their Own Words: A History of the American Negro, Time of Trial, Time of Hope: The Negro in America, 1919-1941, Thaddeus Stevens and the Fight for Negro Rights,* and *Black Magic: A Pictorial History of the Negro* in *American Entertainment,* again with Langston Hughes. His books about Jews include *Remember the Days: A Short History of the Jewish American, Taking Root: Jewish Immigrants in America, The Jewish American: A History in Their Own Words,* and the much honored *Never to Forget: The Jews of the Holocaust.* Workers' interests are explored in *Bread—and Roses: The Struggle of American Labor, 1865-1915* and *Violins and Shovels: The WPA Arts Projects.* Other books treat Chinese Americans, Hispanic Americans, and Native Americans. His biographies of women include those on Lydia Maria Child, Margaret Sanger, Dorothea Lange, Betty Friedan, Winnie Mandela, and Mary McLeod Bethune.

Meltzer's literary honors are almost too numerous to list. Two of his books have won the Jane Addams Peace Association Children's Book Award: *Never to Forget* and *Ain't Gonna Study War No More: The Story of America's Peaceseekers,* and a third, *The Eye of Conscience: Photographers and Social Change,* was named an honor book. His *All Times, All Peoples: A World History of Slavery* was an American Book Award finalist and several others were National Book Award finalists. He has also won the Christopher Award, the Thomas Alva Edison Mass Media Award, and the Jefferson Cup Award, among many others.

Consistently, Meltzer's books are soundly researched and written with style that separates them from the turgid history and superficial biography that has characterized much of children's nonfiction. His has been a voice for the downtrodden and the overlooked, a welcome addition to American children's literature.

Books by Milton Meltzer

A Pictorial History of the Negro in America. With Langston Hughes. New York: Crown, 1956. 6th edition. With C. Eric Lincoln.
A Pictorial History of Black Americans, 1990.
Mark Twain Himself. New York: Crowell, 1960.
A Light in the Dark: The Life of Samuel Gridley Howe. New York: Crowell, 1964.
In Their Own Words: A History of the American Negro, 1619-1865, Vol. I. New York: Crowell, 1964; *1865-1916,* Vol.II. New York: Crowell, 1965; *1916-1966,* Vol. III. New York: Crowell, 1967; ab., *The Black Americans: A History in Their Own Words, 1619-1983.* New York: Crowell, 1984; 1987.
Tongue of Flame: The Life of Lydia Maria Child. New York: Crowell, 1965.
Time of Trial, Time of Hope: The Negro in America, 1919-1941. With August Meier. New York: Doubleday, 1966.
Thaddeus Stevens and the Fight for Negro Rights. New York: Crowell, 1967.
Black Magic: A Pictorial History of the Negro in American Entertainment. With L. Hughes. New York: Prentice-Hall, 1967.
Bread—and Roses: The Struggle of American Labor, 1865-1915. New York: Knopf, 1967.
Langston Hughes: A Biography. New York: Crowell, 1968.
Brother, Can You Spare a Dime? The Great Depression, 1929-1933. New York: Knopf, 1969.
Margaret Sanger: Pioneer of Birth Control. New York: Crowell, 1969.
Freedom Comes to Mississippi: The Story of Reconstruction. Chicago: Follett, 1970.
Slavery: From the Rise of Western Civilization to the Renaissance. New York: Cowles, 1971.
Slavery: From the Renaissance to Today. New York: Cowles, 1972.
To Change the World: A Picture History of Reconstruction. New York: Scholastic, 1971.

Underground Man. New York : Bradbury, 1972; San Diego: Harcourt, 1990.
Hunted Like a Wolf: The Story of the Seminole War. New York: Farrar, 1972.
The Right to Remain Silent. New York: Harcourt, 1972.
The Eye of Conscience: Photographers and Social Change. With Bernard Cole. Chicago: Follett, 1974.
World of Our Fathers: The Jews of Eastern Europe. New York: Farrar, 1974.
Remember the Days: A Short History of the Jewish American. New York: Doubleday, 1974.
Bound for the Rio Grande: The Mexican Struggle 1845-1850. New York: Knopf, 1974.
Taking Root: Jewish Immigrants in America. New York: Farrar, 1974.
Violins and Shovels: The WPA Arts Projects. New York: Delacorte, 1974.
Never to Forget: The Jews of the Holocaust. New York: Harper, 1976.
Dorothea Lange: A Photographer's Life. New York: Farrar, 1978.
The Human Rights Book. New York: Farrar, 1979.
All Times, All Peoples: A World History of Slavery. New York: Harper, 1980.
The Chinese Americans. New York: Crowell, 1980.
The Truth about the Ku Klux Klan. New York: Watts, 1982.
The Hispanic Americans. New York: Crowell, 1982.
The Jewish Americans: A History in Their Own Words, 1650- 1950. New York: Crowell, 1982.
The Terrorists. New York: Harper, 1983.
A Book about Names. New York: Crowell, 1984.
Ain't Gonna Study War No More: The Story of America's Peacemakers. New York: Harper, 1985.
Mark Twain: A Writer's Life. New York: Watts, 1985.
Betty Friedan: A Voice for Women's Rights. New York: Viking, 1985.
Dorothea Lange: Life through the Camera. New York: Viking, 1985.
The Jews in America: A Picture Album. New York: Jewish Pub. Society, 1985.
Poverty in America. New York: Morrow, 1986.
Winnie Mandela: The Soul of South Africa. New York: Viking, 1986.
George Washington and the Birth of Our Nation. New York: Watts, 1986.

Mary McLeod Bethune: Voice of Black Hope. New York: Viking, 1987.
The Landscape of Memory. New York: Viking, 1987.
The American Revolutionaries: A History in Their Own Words, 1750-1800. New York: Crowell, 1987.
Benjamin Franklin: The New American. New York: Watts, 1988.
Rescue: The Story of How Gentiles Saved Jews in the Holocaust. New York: Harper, 1988.
Starting from Home: A Writer's Beginnings; A Memoir by Milton Meltzer. New York: Viking, 1988.
American Politics: How It Really Works. New York: Morrow, 1989.
Voices from the Civil War: A Documentary History of the Great American Conflict. New York: Crowell, 1989.
The American Promise: Voices of A Changing Nation, 1945-Present. New York: Bantam, 1990.
The Bill of Rights: How We Got It and What It Means. New York: Crowell, 1990.
Thomas Jefferson, The Revolutionary Aristocrat. New York: Watts, 1991.

Milton Meltzer's *Brother, Can You Spare a Dime?*: A Study of Passionate Fact

E. Wendy Saul

Those of us who studied literature in the nineteen sixties and seventies were trained to recognize and discuss "excellence" in fiction, poetry, and drama. Although DeTocqueville, Boswell, Johnson, Emerson, and Thoreau made their way into the historical medley of texts presented to us, in courses which focused on "modern" literature, works of nonfiction were virtually absent.

To much of the world fiction seemed like a frill, a form of self-indulgence. As we argued that literary truths were no less significant or real than the facts reported in a daily newspaper, I fear that we ignored authors who used facts to *produce* literary truths. This situation has been somewhat remedied as writers such as John McPhee, Tracy Kidder, Tom Wolfe, and Joan Didion—the new "literary journalists"—are studied in literature courses and receive major national awards. It is with a critical respect for the power of creative nonfiction that I draw attention to a children's author whose work is surely in that same tradition of literary journalism. Milton Meltzer's *Brother, Can You Spare a Dime?* is a book which successfully forges cultural understanding out of passionate fact.

The subject of *Brother, Can You Spare a Dime?* , the economic chaos and despair loosed upon Americans living during the late twenties and early thirties, is key to an understanding of the body (and soul) of Meltzer's work. In his own words:

The unending struggle to realize the promise of America is the theme of all of my writing. My books have to do with men and women who have been movers and shakers, and with the conflicts and crises that mark man's striving for freedom and fulfillment. Why this? Perhaps because I grew up in the years of the Great Depression, had to live on relief for a while, and then worked on WPA. That and service in World War II gave me whatever focus I have. (Commire 157)

Meltzer begins *Brother, Can You Spare a Dime?* with a statement about human memory. He suggests that if young people wish to understand their parents and their grandparents they need to do more than listen to personal reminiscences; they must also understand the history that underpins individual verbalizations:

Half of the people in America today are too young to remember the Great Depression of the 1930's. Their parents remember, and certainly their grandparents. Whether they were rich or poor, bankers or laborers, they remember. Probably they never talk about the "good old days." They don't like to recall the bad days. Not when the days became weeks and months and years, and years, and years. Years that made wounds that never healed. (3)

It has been twenty years since Meltzer penned these words and parents of young readers—the next generation—cannot recall the events he chronicles. And yet the story Meltzer tells, the story shaped out of diaries, photographs, songs, newspaper clips, jokes, and personal recollections, as well as more traditional sources, is a story that all children and adults should hear. Part of what he seeks to convey is relatively concrete: human welfare is affected by big business. Other bits of advice might be better defined as value lessons: security and comfort cannot be guaranteed by hard work alone. Equally important, his message suggests a process for thinking about current and future events: in evaluating explanation one must attend to the purpose of the speaker as much as to the nature of what is being said.

But all this information, all these lessons, are born from stories, layered tales of people trying to maintain their dignity and self-respect through the most difficult of times. Each vignette shines light upon another aspect of the struggle. In 1931 Louis Stark, a reporter, visits the New York City Free Employment Bureau and finds the place packed with conscientious, hungry workers waiting for a job announcement, any job announcement. When the telephone finally rings,

> There is a movement in the crowd... Half a dozen men squirm out. They throw themselves at desk Number 2. Work, blessed blessing, is within their grasp, perhaps. They overwhelm the clerk with a torrent of appeals.
> "Please, mister, I'm a good mechanic."
> "Please, I gotta family."
> "Gimme a chance."
> Swiftly the clerk selects two men. The lucky competitors dash from the room with the precious cards in their fists, each hoping to "beat the other fellow to it." Two are sent for each job listed so that the employer may have a choice.
> The clerk turns back to his desk. With leaden feet the four disappointed men move slowly back and merge again with the patient mass. A thousand desperate souls—minus two—freeze again into a mute appeal. Until a telephone again rings. (70)

But Meltzer does more in this book than collect and arrange stories. He provides a vision and language that enables the reader to frame and share experience. Those of us concerned with issues of justice during the late sixties may recall a tendency to polarize; one's position on the war in Vietnam was the basic sorting mechanism used to judge the correctness of a person's politics. But in 1969, when issues of race, class and gender were generally subordinated to a stance on the war, Meltzer wrote a book about another of America's hard times. In no uncertain terms he portrayed individual and collective desperation, and then pointed the way toward healing. He invited readers to see that a nation can mend herself, although scars surely remain.

Twenty years later, I, the beneficiary of important historical, sociological, anthropological, and literary insights, reread *Brother, Can You Spare a Dime?* Amazingly, the portrait of the Depression painted by Meltzer appears as sensitive, knowledgeable, and relevant today as it was in 1969. The great men and important events of the era are expertly outlined, but the interest and shading of the portrait, its impact, emanates from Meltzer's descriptions of poor, powerless Americans, of women and people of color. Although they own little of material value in America, in the story of the Great Depression they own more than a fair share.

Thus, it is also Milton Meltzer's story, and he marks it as such not only through the choice and arrangement of incident, but also through his language. Calvin Coolidge is described as a "prim, purse-mouthed Yankee" (6), FDR's polio is portrayed in almost metaphorical terms: "the tragic illness he had endured and surmounted made many feel that, rich though he was, he could understand the suffering and poverty of those who struggled to make a living" (162).

Meltzer's perspective, his reason for writing history, is made abundantly apparent in the book's final pages. On the one hand I congratulate him for producing a work that so ably withstands the "test of time." On the other hand I realize that its timeliness is a function of our nation's continuing inability to care for the poor, the hungry and the homeless. *Brother, Can You Spare a Dime?* concludes:

> The gap [between the richest and the poorest] is still there—and it is a dangerous social fact. The resources of our country are rich enough to rescue the generations of poor the Great Depression left behind. A war on poverty is not a new idea. But revolts in the ghettos and marches on Washington show that it has not yet been waged with the will and the daring simple justice demands. (168)

Milton Meltzer's writing is designed to "provide readers with courage," to "give them the heart to strive to make (the world) better" (Meltzer 157). *Brother, Can You Spare a Dime?* is in itself an act of caring. The suffering of the past is made present. As information becomes revelation we find ourselves more able to recognize and realize a humane America.

Works Cited

Commire, Anne. *Something about the Author.* Vol. I. Detroit: Gale Research Co., 1971.
Meltzer, Milton. "The Social Responsibility of the Writer." *The New Advocate,* 22, No. 3 (1989): 155-157.

1989 Phoenix Award Honor Book

Pistol

Adrienne Richard

Adrienne Richard

World traveler, participant in archaeological investigations, and student of traditional cultures, Adrienne Richard has used her interest in the effects of periods on people who lived in those times to shape her writings. In addition to four novels for middle school and young adult readers dealing with the interaction of events and people, she has published articles, short stories, travel sketches, reviews, and the script for an educational film, "Leonardo da Vinci."

Born in Evanston, Illinois, in 1921, Richard grew up in Arizona and Illinois. After receiving her degree from the University of Chicago, she did graduate work at the University of Iowa and Boston College. She has traveled extensively in India, Kuwait, Egypt, and Israel, where she worked on archaeological digs. Her experiences in the Middle East provided the background for *The Accomplice*, a novel about a boy on a dig with his father in contemporary Israel who becomes involved in an Arab guerrilla plot. Richard's home has been in Massachusetts, along with her husband, James, a management consultant.

Her first novel, *Pistol*, was named at the time of its publication to the Fanfare list by the editors of *The Horn Book Magazine*. Its later selection as a Phoenix honor book bears eloquent testimony to its enduring quality. About a boy growing up in Montana range country during the turbulent times of the early Great Depression, *Pistol* interweaves details of everyday ranch life, economic shock and deprivation, and convincing family situations to produce a strong sense of the period without becoming sentimental, judgmental, or instructive.

In *Wings*, her third novel and a finalist for the National Book Award, Richard also brings the setting vividly to the fore—among a Bohemian crowd of intellectuals and nonconformists in California in 1928. Episodes revolve around an assertive, spirited little girl mad about airplanes, her beautiful, lively mother, and the mother's many eccentric friends. As in *Pistol*, the pace is well regulated, diction literate and vigorous, point of view unerringly accurate, and tone sympathetic, honest, and spiced with gentle humor.

Richard's latest book, *Into the Road,* a contemporary teen novel, also skillfully uses sociology as the basis for a story, combining motorcycle gang subculture and a fractured home. Two orphaned brothers, parted at a young age, become friends while biking with their machines through New England, where they encounter leather-jacket gangs, mobs, and the unique code of the rode.

Although her output has been limited, Richard's books stand forth for their substance, sound basis in fact, strongly realized characters, and warm sensitivity to human problems and concerns. In according honor status to *Pistol,* The Children's Literature Association pays tribute to Adrienne Richard, who, like Rosemary Sutcliff, Leon Garfield, Robert Burch, Erik Haugaard, Helen Cresswell, and Milton Meltzer before her, the Association regards as an accomplished and valued writer for the young.

Books by Adrienne Richard

Pistol. Boston: Little, Brown, 1969; 1989.
The Accomplice. Boston: Little, Brown, 1973.
Wings. Boston: Little, Brown, 1974.
Into the Road. Boston: Little, Brown, 1976.

Pistol:
End of an Era, Beginning of Another

Taimi M. Ranta

One of the two Phoenix Award honor books for 1989 is *Pistol,* a vigorous, distinguished novel by Adrienne Richard. It was published in 1969, the year of *My Darling, My Hamburger* (Zindel), *Sounder* (Armstrong) and *Where the Lilies Bloom* (Cleavers), so-called "ground breaker" books in young adult literature with their bold thrusts in the choice of subject matter, character, language, setting, and mood. *Pistol,* a very perceptive, compelling, adventure-packed novel of a young boy's convincing journey to manhood in a crumbling world, didn't get the attention it deserved then and still deserves today.

Pistol began as a short story based largely on experiences of the author's husband who grew up in southeastern Montana, becoming the core of the "Christmas on Wolf Creek" chapter about driving cattle through a blizzard. She writes that "after that I began to imagine what this boy was like, where he had been and where he was going, what was happening to him and around him" (Commire 157). It became fiction with a strong undergirding of the history of the country and the region in the early years of the Great Depression.

In this intense historical novel, the author ingeniously combines a tautly-woven plot, well-delineated characters, and sharply drawn descriptions of very difficult times. The novel is full of local terms and western pronounciations and mention of the flora and fauna of Montana that add authenticity to the narrative and conversation. Events are seen through the eyes of Billy Catlett, a teenager who lives his high school years in Great Plains, Montana, where his family finally settled after years of crisscrossing the state, following the restless, ineffectual father from job to job. Great Plains is the biggest place yet, a fictitious cow town on the main line of the Northern

Pacific Railroad, population around "eight thousand counting grasshoppers and critters," and, as Billy feels, "a great town for a boy" (5). Here he witnesses the droughts and the Great Depression disabling his state, drastically changing the life of everyone he knows.

This first person narrative is divided into two parts—Sunup and Sundown. The first half, Sunup, begins in June, 1930, when fourteen-year old Billy does what every boy in town wants to do, that is, signs up as a young wrangler, a "pistol" in cowboy slang for "boy." Summers in Sam Tolliver's outfit are "a perfect world, a perfect life" (41). Billy learns to ride circle, round up cattle, brand calves, gentle a wild pony, fight a brush fire, and take with admirable composure the joking and teasing of the older hands. It also includes his first gentle love, Allison Mitchell, daughter of a rich rancher.

The second half, Sundown, tells of the hard years after the Depression staggers the state, the local bank folds, businesses close, people leave to search for work elsewhere, ranchers go broke, Sam himself is ruined, Mr. Catlett's meatpacking plant fails, and the family's belongings are repossessed. Mr. Catlett soon runs away to look for work. Conrad, Billy's older bright, aggressive brother, always rebellious against his father, becomes even more cynical and distant. For the first time, Billy becomes acutely aware of his fragile, kind, quiet mother and her needs and concerns.

Since work on the ranch is no longer available, Billy helps in a gas station, and his brother washes dishes to supplement the meager money their mother has stashed away in an old sock. Soon after Billy graduates from high school, the father returns and moves his family to a crude boom town on the Missouri River where the federal government is constructing a large dam. The men find jobs, but the terrified mother seldom leaves their tarpaper shack. Here Billy and Conrad come to some understanding and the father finally faces reality. After a year of making money at the dam site, they return to Great Plains. Conrad and Billy both have dreams. Conrad wants to settle down in Montana and hopes to have his own ranch some day. Billy decides he must see something of the world and signs up as a cow-puncher, taking cattle to the big cities. He doesn't know where he'll go or what he will do, but he looks forward to the adventure.

As the story ends on September, 1934, Pistol is precariously perched alone on top of the old red Pullman, the eating-living-sleeping car for the men. Behind him, parallel tracks reach back to where his home town and boyhood have vanished. Ahead of him snakes the string of cattle cars preceded by the chugging steam engine, the tracks leading to the new horizon. In many westerns, the cowboy rides his favorite horse westward into the sunset, but Pistol is riding the rails eastward to an unknown but beckoning future which is, as he says, "beyond the horizon of my knowledge." As his eye sweeps in the stretch of prairie, he smiles. "Excitement caught my lung" is all he can say (245).

The *Bulletin of the Center for Children's Books* considered *Pistol* "an unusual setting for an unusual depression era story in a book that is distinguished by honesty, sensitivity and some delightful scenes of cowboy humor" (116).

Horn Book felt the author "tells Billy's story with such conviction that the reader feels the writer has walked in Billy Catlett's boots" (679).

Publishers Weekly stated, "It is impossible to visualize a boy who will not like *Pistol*. Boys will like it for the obvious reason that it is the story of a young wrangler . . . and his wild pony, and for the more subtle reason that boys are apt to admire courage above all other virtues" (85). Girls, too, will read *Pistol*. With the recent wider acceptance of the whole language approach, interest in climactic units has increased. Survival books form a subgenre popular with most middle school through high school students. Courage is another well-received focus. *Pistol* is a worthy selection for both. Sometimes *Pistol* is called a "western" or "cowboy" novel. It is both, of course, but also far more than implied in these designations. It is a powerful rite of passage story, a boy becoming a man. This, too, could be the focal novel in a unit on such books.

Pistol deals unsurprisingly with some of life's harsh realities, but the author convincingly manages an affirmative, open-ended conclusion. Since the story is open ended, the reader can only conjecture what will happen to Billy Catlett in the future. Will he be reunited with Allison, his first love? Not likely. However, he is a flexible individual. He has already adjusted to many different people, situations, and circumstances. He'll make it!

Adrienne Richard has noted that "Those moments in history that strike me with greatest force are watershed moments when everything is changing fast" (Holtze 260). In conclusion, it is important to note that *Pistol* stands on the line between the older junior novels and the birth of new realism in literature for adolescents. It depicts the exciting years of a boy poised on the threshold of young manhood at a watershed period in American history, the Great Depression.

Works Cited

Commire, Anne. *Something About the Author.* Vol. 5. Detroit: Gale Research, 1973.
Evory, Ann. *Contemporary Authors.* Vol. 29-32, rev. ed. Detroit: Gale Research, 1978.
Holtze, Sally Holmes, ed. "Adrienne Richard." *Fifth Book of Junior Authors and Illustrators.* New York: H. W. Wilson, 1983.
Long, Sidney D. Rev. of *Pistol,* by Adrienne Richard. *The Horn Book Magazine* 45 (1969): 679.
Rev. of *Pistol,* by Adrienne Richard. *Bulletin of the Center for Children's Books* 23 (1970): 116.
Rev. of *Pistol,* by Adrienne Richard. *Publishers Weekly* 196 (September 22, 1969): 85.

About the Editors

Alethea Helbig, Professor, and Agnes Perkins, Professor Emeritus, both of English Language and Literature at Eastern Michigan University, have taught and published in children's literature for many years and were instrumental in initiating master's and undergraduate programs in children's literature at Eastern Michigan. They are authors of a series of encyclopedic works on fiction for children published by Greenwood Press: *Dictionary of American Children's Fiction* (two vols.), *Dictionary of British Children's Fiction* (two vols.), and *Dictionary of Children's Fiction from Australia, Canada, India, New Zealand, and Selected African Countries*. They are also compilers (with Helen Hill) of *Straight on Till Morning: Poems of the Imaginary World* and *Dusk to Dawn: Poems of Night* (both Crowell). In addition, Perkins has compiled (with Hill) *New Coasts and Strange Harbors: Discovering Poems* (Crowell). Helbig is also author of *Nanabozhoo, Giver of Life* (Green Oak Press) and is a past president of The Children's Literature Association. They have both published numerous articles on children's literature and are currently working on supplements to the dictionaries of children's fiction and a book on multicultural imaginative literature for young people.